# LOST COUNTRY HOUSES OF CUMBRIA



IAN GREAVES AND
EMILY OSBORNE

AMBERLEY

This edition first published 2026

Amberley Publishing
The Hill, Stroud
Gloucestershire GL5 4EP

www.amberley-books.com



British Library Cataloguing in Publication Data.
A catalogue record for this book is available from the British Library.

ISBN 978 1 3981 2099 0 (print)
ISBN 978 1 3981 2100 3 (ebook)

Typesetting by Hurix Digital, India.
Printed in Great Britain.

Appointed GPSR EU Representative: Easy Access System Europe Oü, 16879218
Address: Mustamäe tee 50, 10621, Tallinn, Estonia
Contact Details: gpsr.requests@easproject.com, +358 40 500 3575

# Introduction

This is the fourth in a series of books describing the lost country houses of the north of England. It covers what is now Cumbria but was, for centuries, Cumberland, Westmorland, and Furness in Lancashire. This area includes the Lake District, the northern shore of Morecambe Bay and the west coast and stretches to the Scottish border and the western margin of Yorkshire. Most of this area was contested land shaped by its proximity to Scotland and until the early eighteenth century, defence was the primary aspiration of its landed families. Defensive towers, peles, scatter the landscape, often with a hall alongside or in a typical tower-hall-tower arrangement. As a result, perhaps the biggest challenge has been to decide what constitutes a country house, especially in relation to the numerous peles in various states of preservation. In order to achieve some control and coherence, therefore, we have only included fortified houses (and indeed castles) if, at some point in their history, they were enlarged into a substantial mansion which has subsequently been demolished; those which survive as farmhouses and were never bigger than a defended manor are not included. Many houses by tradition are said to have been based around a defensive tower, but not infrequently there seems to be little evidence to support this beyond a desire to establish a more ancient foundation for a property. Similarly, in the nineteenth century, Lancashire industrial wealth and social aspirations produced a rash of pretend peles designed to add historical heft to new money.

The nature of the landscape of Cumbria and especially of the Lake District means that country houses, existing or lost, are relatively few in number. Cumbria's pastoral landscape is carved up by the mountainous areas of the Lakes to the west and the North Pennines to the east, areas that were largely inhospitable to country seats and estates. Perhaps the only family that might be considered magnates on a national scale are the Lowthers, without their castle perhaps, but still ensconced in the north-east Lake District after approaching a thousand years. Only a handful of the peles became great houses: Sizergh Castle and Hutton-in-the-Forest are examples of such buildings that survive. Those that didn't are included in the book.

A second, much bigger group of houses includes the ancient seats of minor or middling gentry. Amongst the losses here are Brayton, Crofton and Eden halls. With the development of the Lake District as a tourist destination in the nineteenth century, many new houses were built, often to take advantage of the views, by wealthy industrialists, businessmen or brewers. The losses in this group are the greatest by comparison, although had they lasted a little longer, more might have found salvation as hotels or institutions. New nineteenth-century wealth, most commonly from mining, on occasion resulted in a spasm of enlargement of earlier seats, and of these, two, Lowther and Brougham are discussed in the book and survive, albeit as conserved ruins. Most of these losses were of large, unlovely and entirely impractical mansions unsupported by adequate landholdings or built on the proceeds of transient business or professional success. The Lake Counties for centuries were home to a society with much less social hierarchy than might be found elsewhere; until relatively recently many rural areas were miniature democracies where long-established statesman-farmers cooperated to run their communities: there was a hierarchy, but one which was, in general, much flatter and based on relatively small landholdings. This structure has undoubtedly reduced the number of status houses from which the lost houses might be selected. Only round the edges of the area did the larger estates flourish. On the west coast increasing, and now vanished, industrialisation and coal mining first funded and then destroyed a number of significant country houses. There has never been a Cumbrian Chatsworth or Castle Howard and no house of this status or significance has been lost or will be found in this book. This is not to say that the lost houses were unimportant. Many reflected the fortunes of families prominent in local life for centuries; some, most notably Brayton and Lowther, *did* hold important collections. The fortunes of the most significant lost houses have varied dramatically and unexpectedly over recent years: despite its gift to the local council as a civic asset, Workington Hall, the ancient seat of the Curwens, was allowed to fall into decay and was gutted but conserved as a ruin; Brayton Hall with its nationally important library has gone completely; Lowther Castle, as a result of the foresight of the Lowther family, has been stabilised, partially restored and is now a major tourist attraction; Brougham Castle has been partly restored and is now home to a craft community, although its partial demolition was sufficiently thorough to prevent its complete restoration; and all that remains of Eden Hall, ancient seat of the Musgraves, are the lodge, gate piers and home farm. The Luck of Edenhall, an ancient glass vessel, survives in the Victoria and Albert Museum and is an example of a particularly local phenomenon which will be described in detail.

The lost houses included in this book represent as complete a list as we have been able to establish and validate. If readers know of any others, we would be delighted to hear about them. We would also be grateful for pictures of those houses where we have been unable to locate an illustration. Despite exhaustive efforts we have been able to locate illustrations of Cockermouth Old Hall, Cleator Hall and Distington Hall. As in previous volumes, we have included the odd folk tale or ghost story associated with the houses we discuss, and also, in brief, the histories of some of the great families associated with the turbulent history of the western border counties. Here are tales of Lowthers, Curwens and Musgraves, border reivers, industrialists and eccentrics and many others, representing a fascinating aspect of the history of this dramatic county. It is also worth ending on a positive note: Lowther Castle has resumed its place at the heart of the local community and economy; High Head and Brougham are in safe hands; Kirklinton is being restored; and Dalton Hall remains in the same family and has been replaced by a new and distinguished house on a smaller scale. The vigour of the area as a tourist destination makes further losses unlikely.

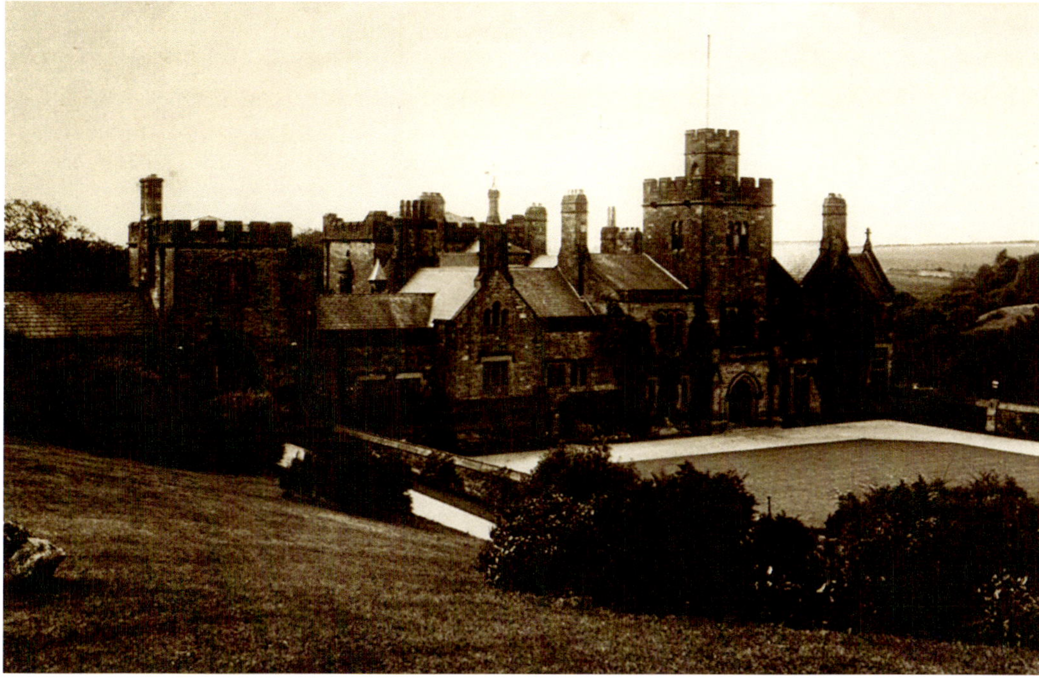

The entrance front of Abbot's Wood.

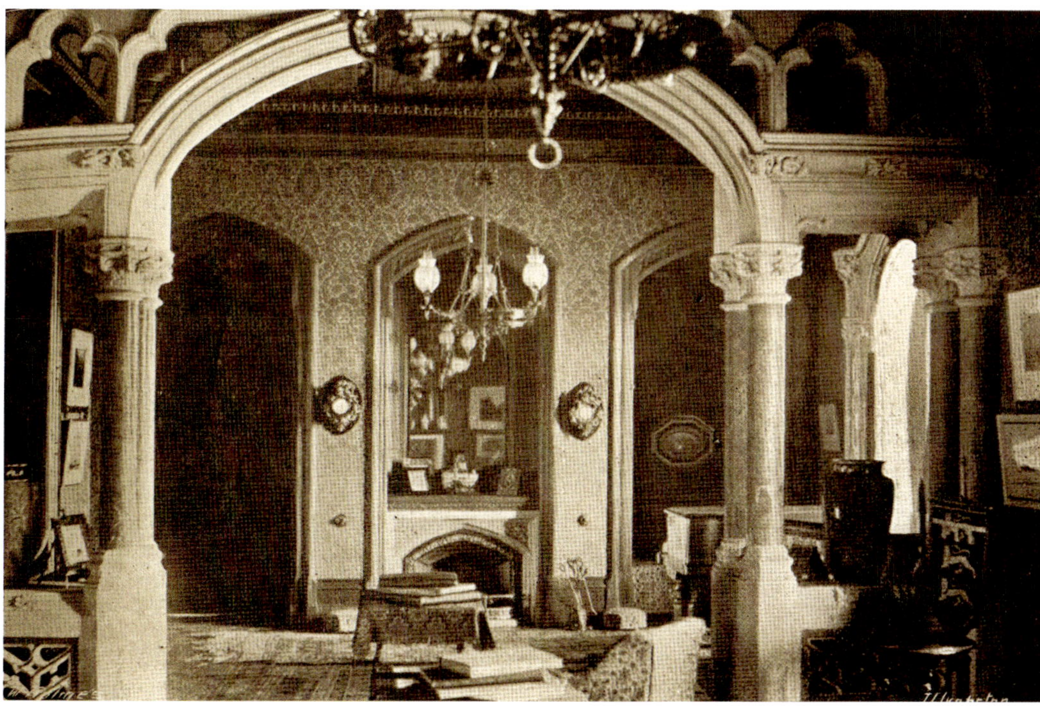

The saloon of Abbot's Wood.

## Abbot's Wood, Barrow-in-Furness

Abbot's Wood (also Abbotswood) was a rambling irregular house on a grand scale with lots of medieval detail, built by the Furness Railway between 1857 and 1859 for Sir James Ramsden, the 'Father of Barrow', to designs by Edward Paley. The building cost £2,000 and Sir James occupied it for a rent of £205 a year. When he died in 1896 the house and estate passed to his son, Frederick, who died in 1941.

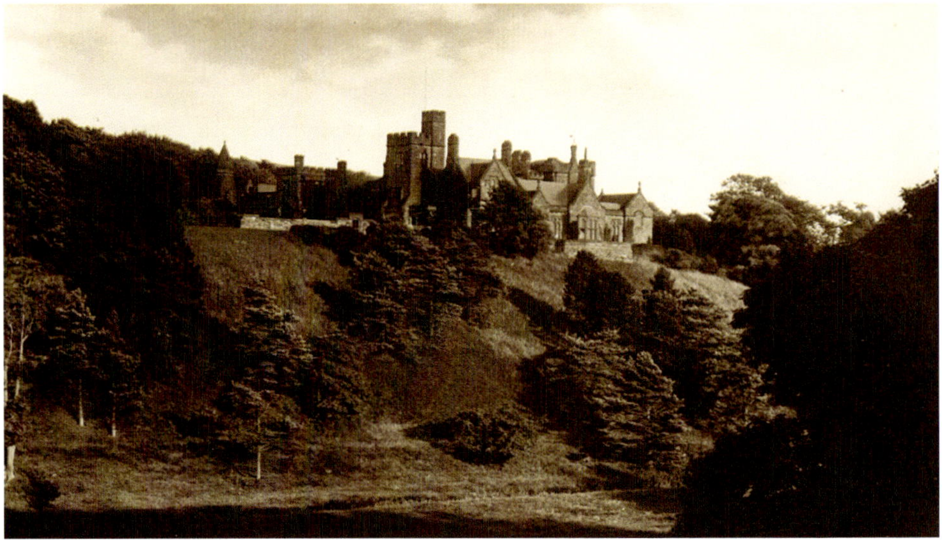

Abbot's Wood.

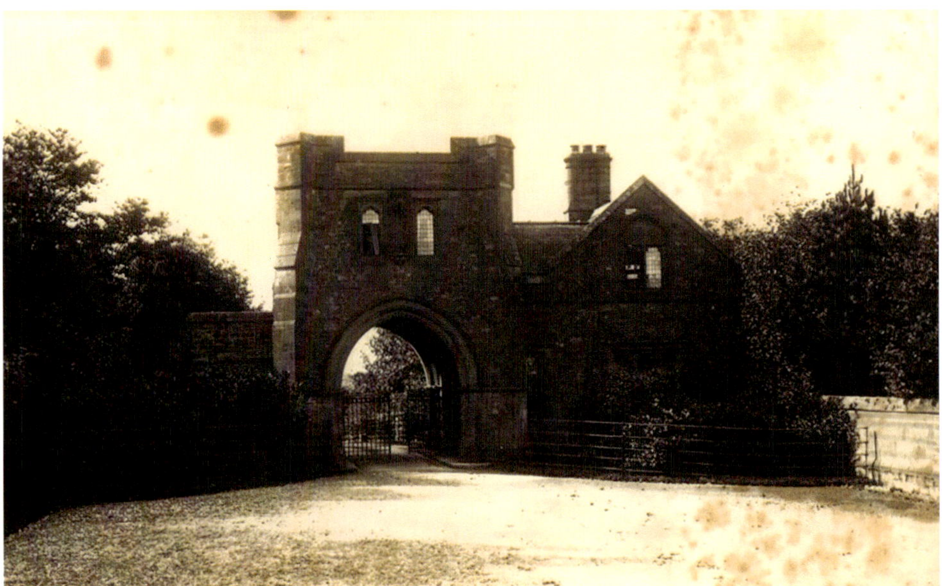

Abbot's Wood North Lodge.

The house was an Army training camp during the Second World War and was later a convalescent home. Abbot's Wood was demolished in 1961. The home farm, lodges and a number of cottages – all by Paley's practice – survive and some of the house's Gillow furniture is in Barrow Town Hall. In the early 1950s a Royal Artillery Anti-Aircraft Operations Room was built in the grounds of Abbot's Wood, one of many constructed around the country in the early days of the Cold War. It has since been demolished. Abbot's Wood's grounds are now a nature reserve.

## Bardsea Hall, Ulverston

Bardsey Hall was the seat of the Roman Catholic (de) Bardsea (Bardsey) family from the Norman Conquest or soon after and there was presumably some form of manor house on the site at an early period. The final Bardsey to own the estate was Nicholas, who in 1558 murdered William Sandys of Conishead, with whom there had been a family dispute regarding tithe corn. Nicholas fled to Scotland, returning seven years later and dying in 1586 having sold the estate. The last of the Bardsey line appears to have been another Nicholas Bardsey, who died in 1643 during the Civil War. The estate passed to Elizabeth Bardsey, who married Christopher Anderson and is recorded living at Bardsea in 1672.

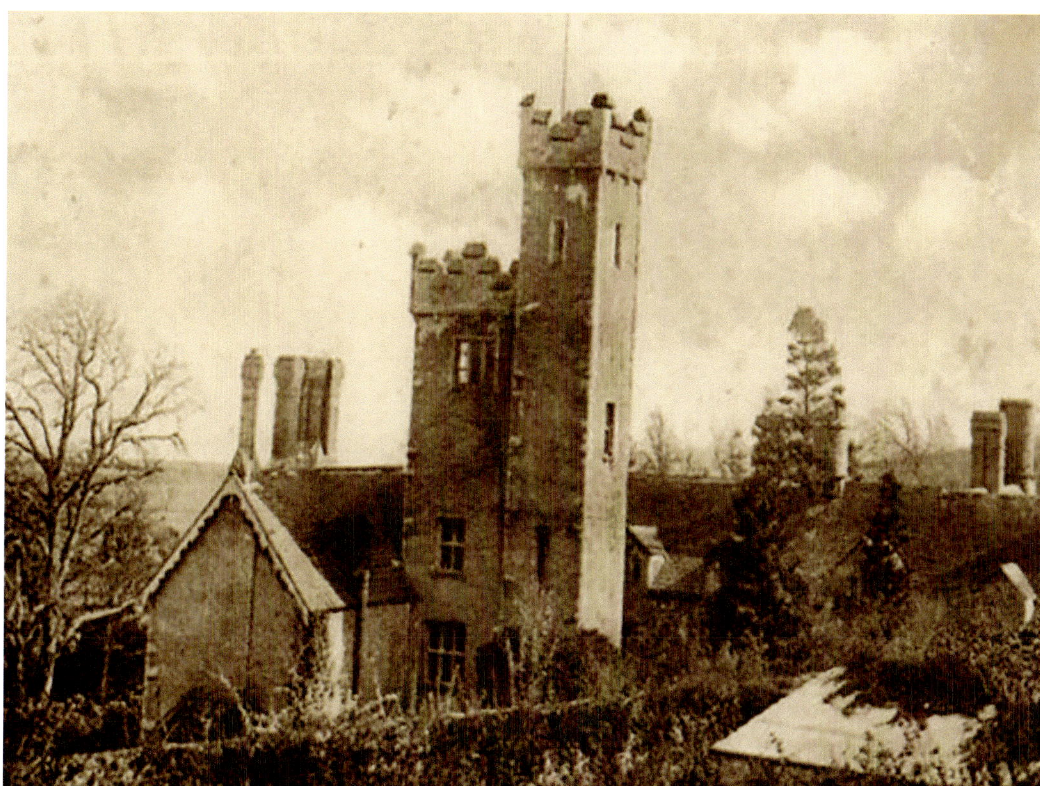

Bardsea Hall.

At the time of the Glorious Revolution (1688), the Jesuit priest at Bardsea Hall, Father Clement Smith, escaped from the house whilst it was under siege by a 300-strong Protestant mob. After a night hidden in local woodland he returned to be hidden in the hall. In the late seventeenth century Lord Molineux purchased the hall for use as a hunting lodge. Soon afterwards it became the property of Christopher Wilson, who married Margaret, daughter of John Braddyll, of Conishead Priory, and from the Wilsons it passed to the Gales in the early nineteenth century. In 1843, Bardsea Hall was said to 'much resemble a Swiss chalet', although any similarity is not evident on a contemporary illustration.

In 1881 Bardsea Hall was home to Henry Richmond Gale and his wife Emma. Their son Wilson Gale took the name Braddyll on inheriting the Conishead estate and his brother Lt General Henry Gale succeeded to the family's original estate. A ruinously expensive reconstruction of Conishead would lead to the sale of that estate in the 1860s.

In its final form Bardsea was an eighteenth-century house remodelled in Jacobethan style with a prominent tower around 1840 by William Gale, and sold by the Braddylls in 1918. Bardsea Hall was demolished in 1927 and modern housing stands on the site. The Bardsea Monument, once a summerhouse sited to enjoy views of the estate and later a monument commemorating members of the Gale and Wilson families, survives near the site of the hall.

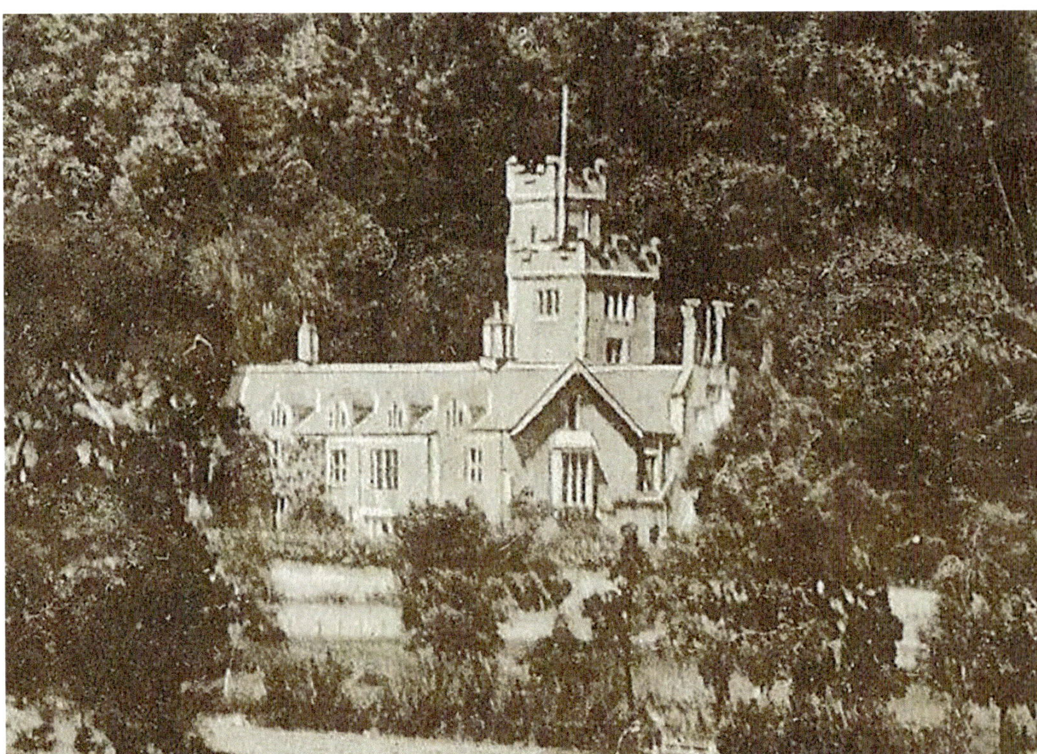

Bardsea Hall.

## Barrow Island (Old Island House, Michaelson House), Barrow-in-Furness

Barrow Island was a seat of the Michaelsons, who acquired it in the eighteenth century, and was also known as Michaelson House. The house was rebuilt around 1730 and in 1851 was described as 'a handsome mansion called *Old Island Hall*, the seat and property of Thos. Y.P. Michaelson, Esq. who is also owner of the whole of the island. This mansion occupies a pleasant situation near the shore, and is finely shaded with trees.' The property was sold to the Furness Railway in 1863 and by 1882 the description had changed to 'the erstwhile pebbly strand is now covered with warehouses, workshops and business premises'. Barrow Island House was demolished at the beginning of the Great War to make room for a factory making howitzers.

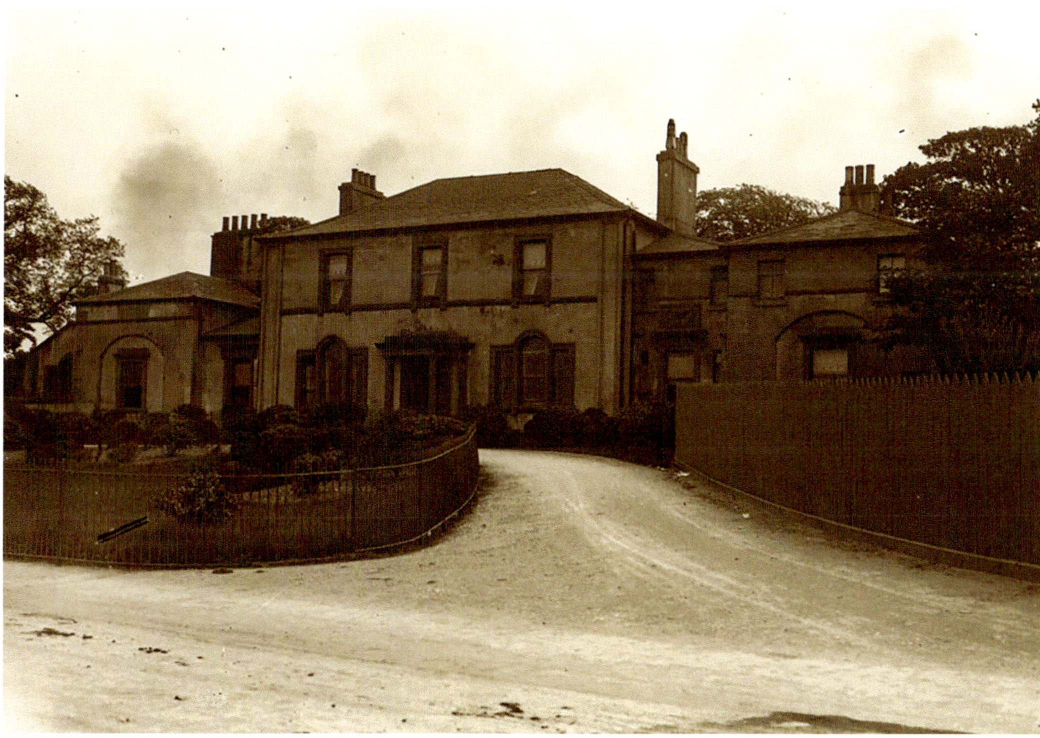

Barrow Island.

## Beetham Hall, Beetham

The Beethams held Beetham Hall for many generations before losing it by fighting on the wrong side at Bosworth in 1485, at which time it passed to the Stanleys. The estate is described by the great sixteenth-century antiquarian John Leland in his *Itinerary*: 'by Bitham is a greate parke and a goodly place yn hit of the Erle of Darby'. Thomas Fairfax captured Beetham from its later Royalist owners in 1644 and it later became a Clifford seat. By 1671 it was described by Sir Daniel Fleming as 'a pleasant seat, and hath been a fair house, but now much ruined'.

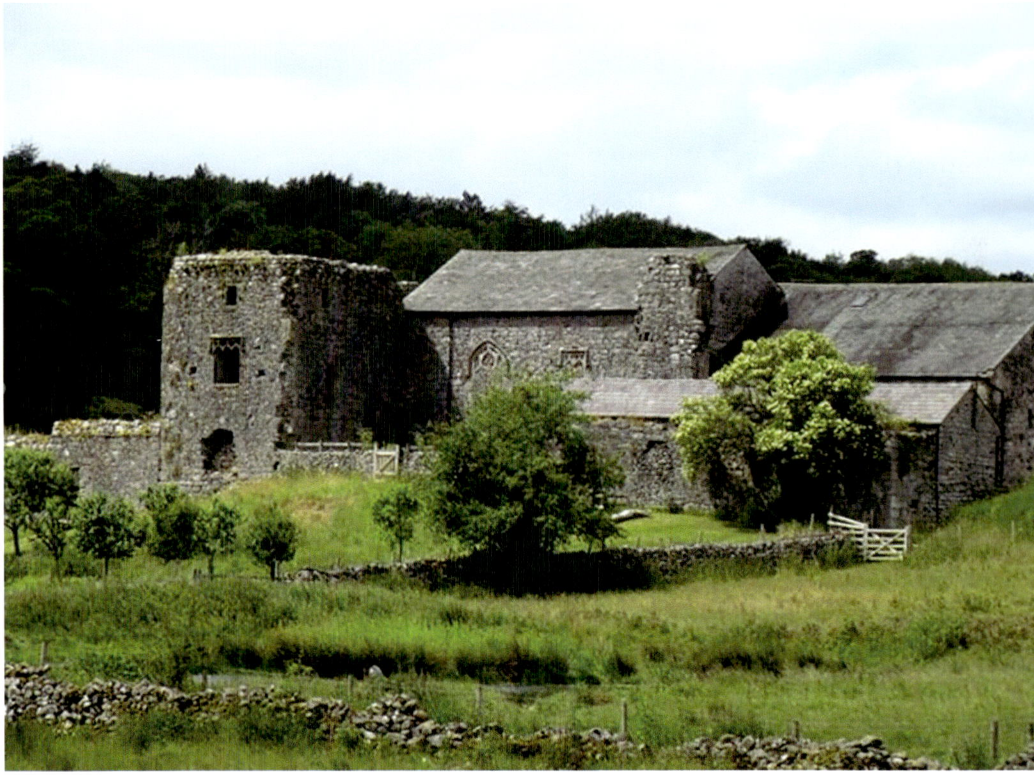

Beetham Hall.

In the shadow of the ruined hall the existing farmhouse was built by Thomas Brabin – who had the lease of the estate – in 1693, as attested by the initials and weathered date on the lintel of an entranceway. From 1700 the house was occupied by George Hilton, a Roman Catholic and sometime Jacobite who fought in the Battle of Preston in 1715. He is notable for his diaries in which he documented his scandalous lifestyle of excess, which involved plenty of drinking, gambling and women.

The Wilsons of Dallam acquired Beetham in 1767. Substantial remains of the manor house are still in situ, now in use as a farm with the attached farmhouse. The domestic block took the conventional local form of a hall, with family rooms and staircase to the upper floor at the high end and service rooms at the lower. Much of the curtain wall is intact and architectural elements of the chapel survive.

## The Biggins, High Biggins

Formerly the property of the Battersby family, the Biggins estate had passed to the Tomlinsons and in 1889 William S. Paget inherited it from his distant cousin Elizabeth Tomlinson. The hall was designed for him by William Verity and constructed by the local builder William Bayliff in 1893 'within 200 yards of the old house'. Also known as Biggins Hall, the Biggins was essentially a longer and lower version of Fountains Hall near Ripon, of which its garden front was almost a copy, including the square towers, pedimented bays and central semicircular oriel, but oddly stretched.

William Paget added the name Tomlinson to his own and lived at the Biggins until his death in 1930. The hall was destroyed by fire whilst in military occupation during the Second World War. The surviving outbuildings include elements of a medieval hall. The Paget-Tomlinsons continued to own the estate into the 1960s.

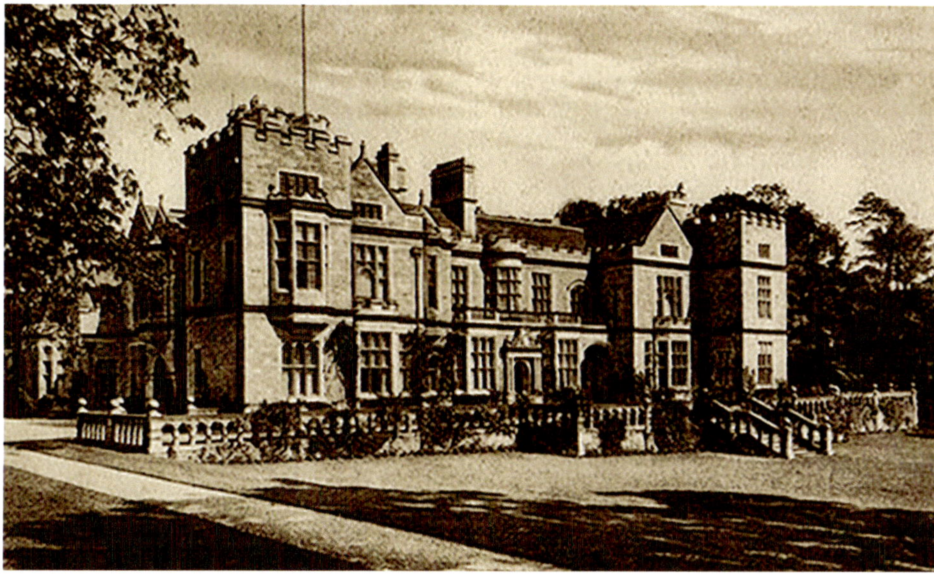

The Biggins.

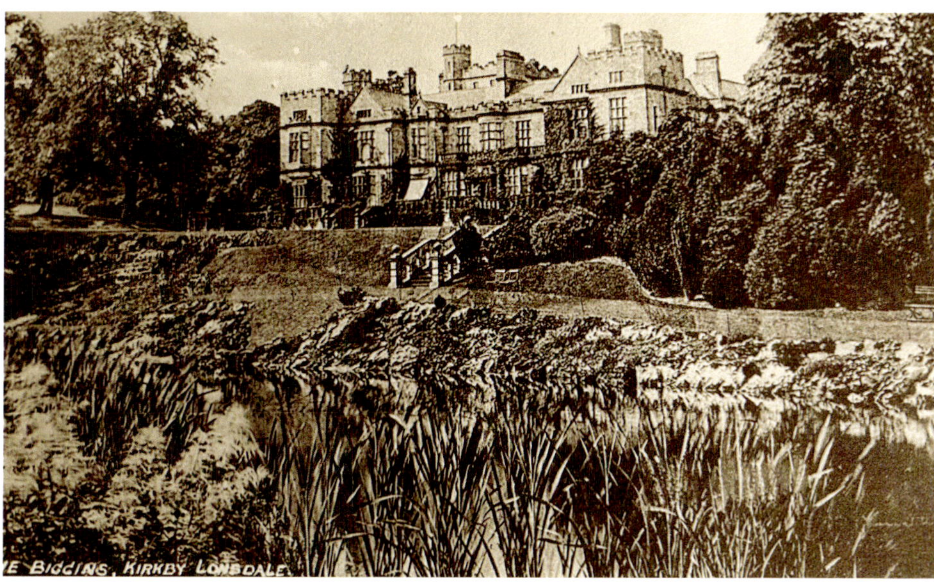


The Biggins.

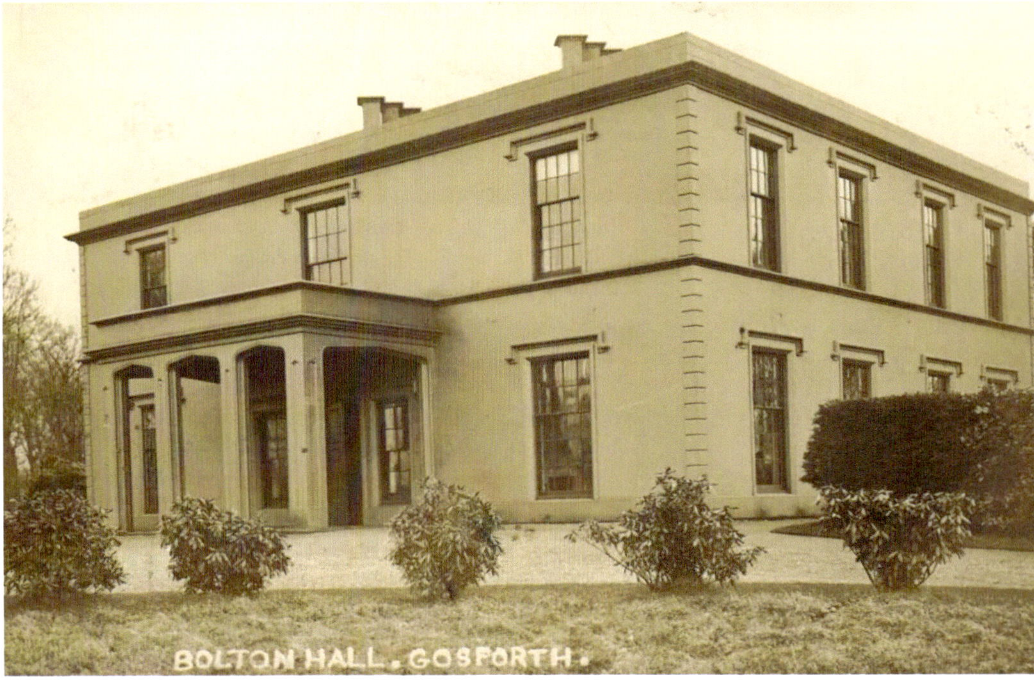


Bolton Hall, Gosforth.

## Bolton Hall (Hall Bolton), Gosforth

Formerly the seat of the Liverpool shipping dynasty, the Brocklebanks, Bolton Hall was demolished in 1951. The Brocklebank Line was founded in Whitehaven in 1785. After amalgamation with Cunard, the last Brocklebank flagged ships were sold in 1983, after almost two hundred years. During the Second World War the hall was used to accommodate Land Girls. It was a very plain rendered villa, three bays by four with a prominent three-arch gothic porch, quoins and drip moulds over the windows. The Brocklebanks would later build Grizedale Hall, which has also been demolished.

## Brandlingill Manor, Cockermouth

Little information is available about Brandlingill, which was demolished in the 1950s due to dry rot and woodworm. The stable block survives. In its final form it appears to have been Victorian, in a vague Jacobethan style including a pretend pele tower, although earlier elements are possible and a lower wing to the rear was probably of an earlier date.

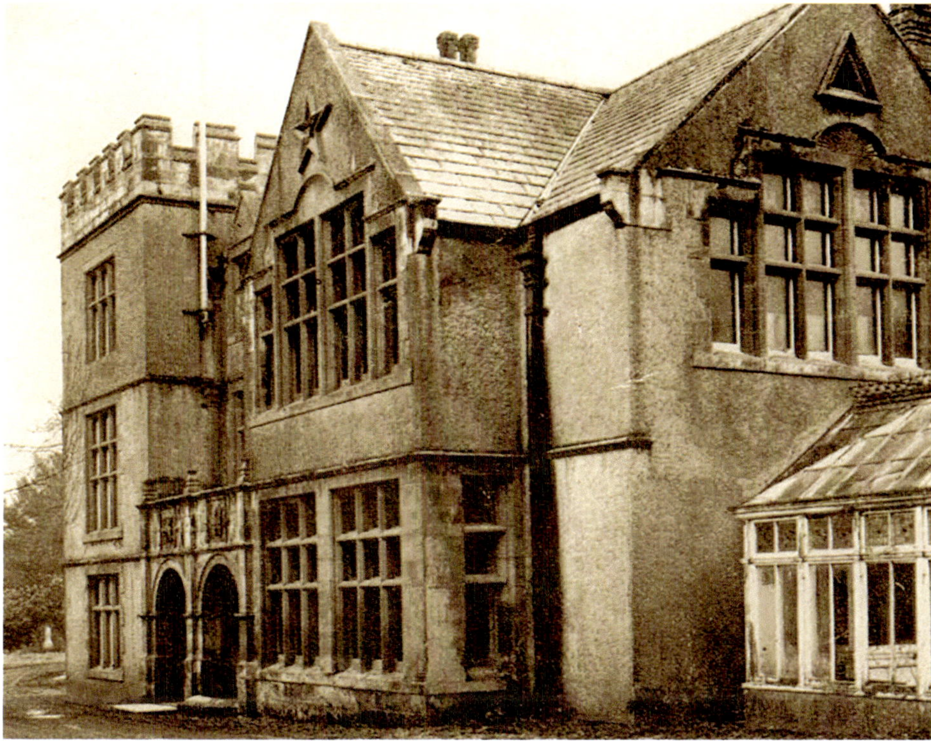

The entrance front of Brandlingill Manor.

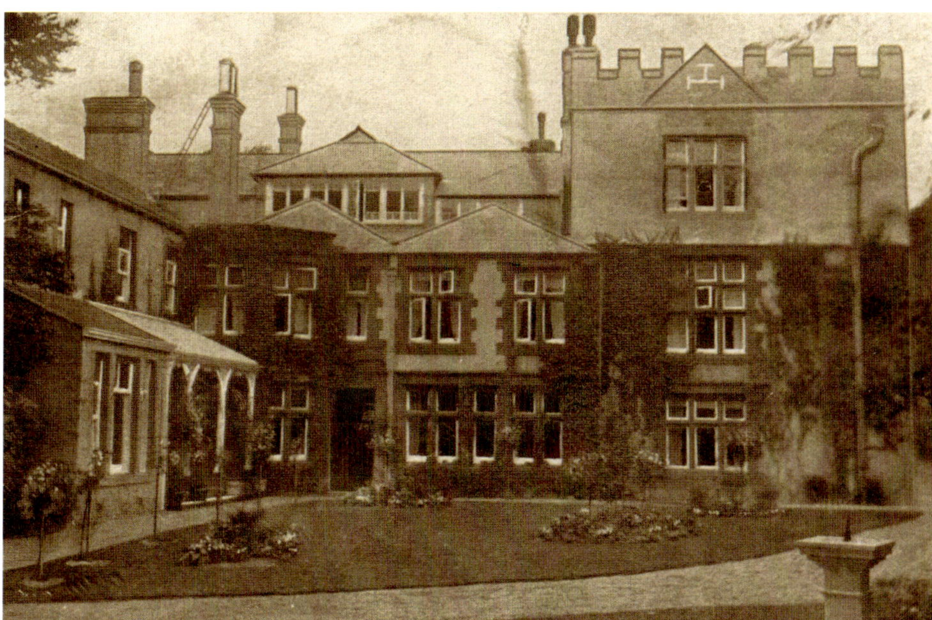

The garden front of Brandlingill.

## Brayton Hall, Aspatria

The vast seat of the Lawsons was almost entirely destroyed by fire in 1940. After the Norman Conquest Brayton was granted to Ughtred; in 1578 William Bewley owned it. Brayton was subsequently the property of a member of the Salkeld family, whose co-heiresses sold it to Sir Wilfrid Lawson, 1st Baronet, in the late eighteenth century.

The Lawsons were descended from the early thirteenth-century John Lawson of Fawkegrave, in Yorkshire. Sir Wilfrid Lawson, who died childless aged eighty-seven in 1632, was steward to the Earl of Northumberland, High Sheriff of Cumberland and the county's MP. His great-nephew Wilfred succeeded him and in 1632 was created baronet of Isel, dividing his estates on his death so that Isel, which Wilfred Lawson senior had acquired by marriage in 1624, passed to his heir, the son of his eldest son and later 2nd Baronet, and Brayton, which he had purchased, to the line of his younger son.

Although there had been a manor house on the estate, this was hugely enlarged in 1800 at the same time as the house's setting was developed. The library held an important collection of works, especially concerning natural history, and there was also a fine picture collection. Shelley used the Lawson's library during his honeymoon. At its peak, the estate extended over more than 6,500 acres.

In 1868, the 2nd Baronet (after the extinction of the first Lawson baronetcy in 1806, it was recreated in 1831 for the Lawsons of Brayton) further enlarged the house, forming a three-storey, stuccoed, stone-built mansion, in the form of a quadrangle enclosing an open court. John Crace designed many of the interiors. A number of the rooms had specific decorative themes including the Maple, Ebony, Bamboo and Sheraton Rooms.

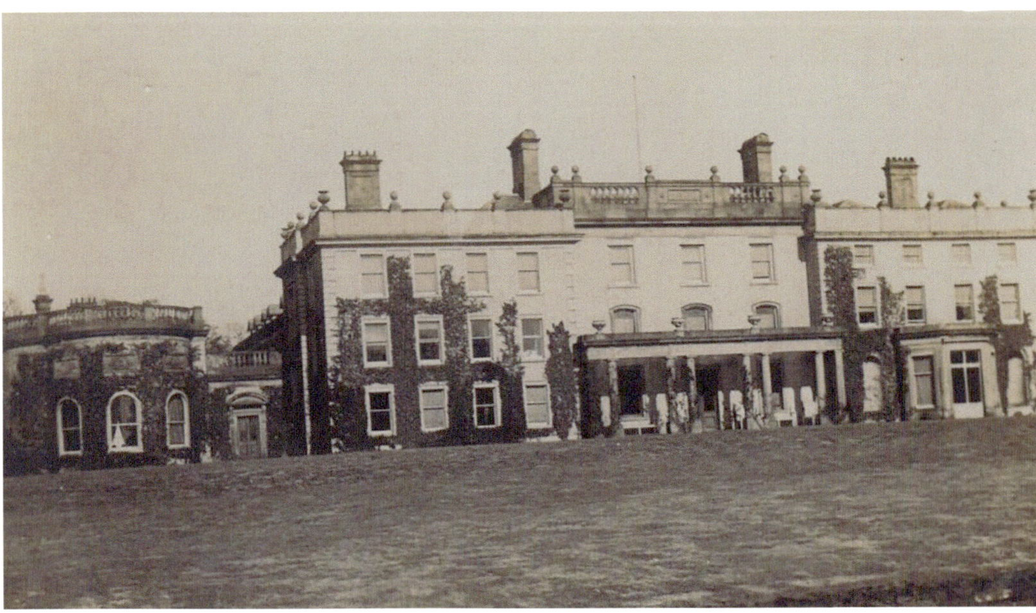

Brayton Hall.

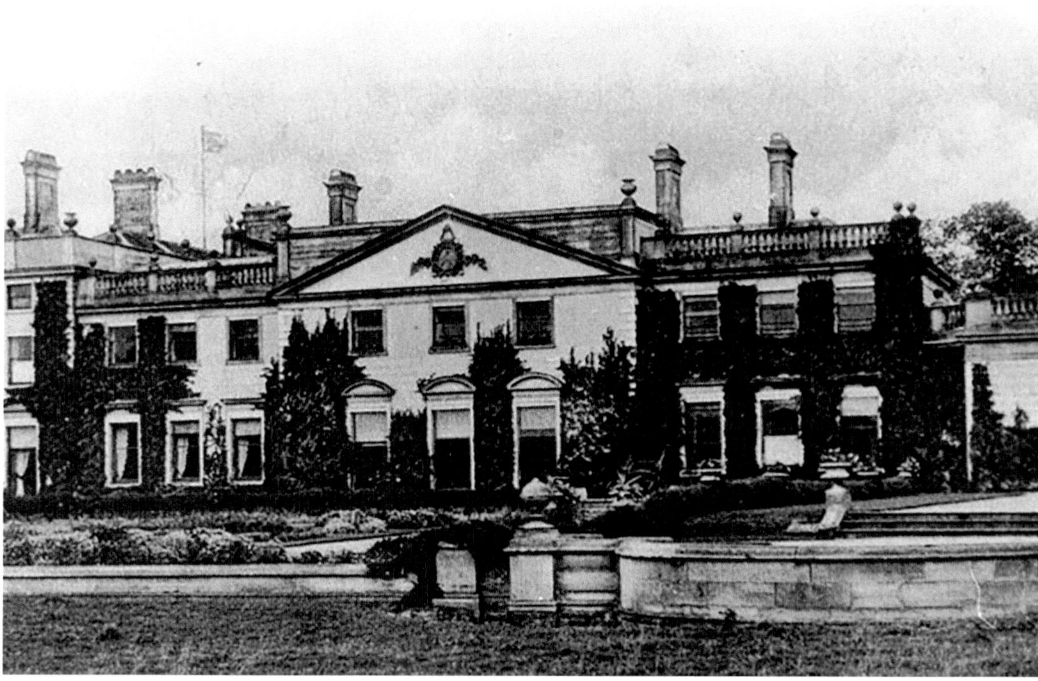

Brayton Hall.

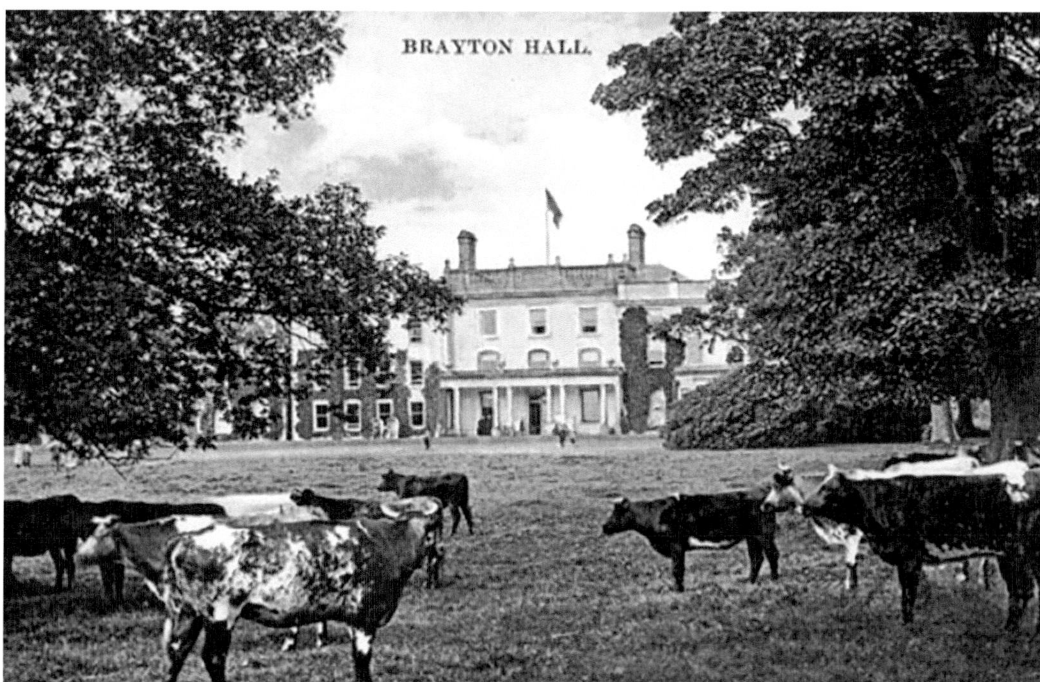


Brayton Hall with shorthorn cattle in the foreground.

The Lawsons allowed public access to their grounds when they were not in residence, occasionally providing a band and allowing skating on the lake in winter. A variety of events were held there, most notably temperance rallies, the 2nd Baronet being a committed advocate of temperance reform.

On 21 September 1918 Brayton Hall was almost entirely destroyed by fire. Most of the accumulated collections of the Lawsons were lost, and only some of the furniture and part of the library were saved. At the time of the fire the 4th Baronet had been living at Isel Hall, leaving Brayton unoccupied most of the time. Having promised Isel to a nephew, preparations were being made for the baronet's return to Brayton. The cause of the fire was never established and only the north wing was saved. This was later incorporated into a smaller house, which still incorporated extensive service rooms and a clover leaf-shaped dining room.

The estate was sold by the Lawsons in 1938 and bought by Henry Dryden Ward. During the Second World War the Brayton Park estate was requisitioned by the RAF. Personnel were billeted in the hall and two runways were built in the park. After the war Henry's son Robert and his wife moved into Home Farm and the hall fell gradually into disrepair. Much of the stonework was used to build a new house in the Wards' home village in County Durham. The estate remains in the Ward family and fragments of the house survive. During its ownership by the Lawsons, Brayton was famous for its herd of shorthorn cattle.

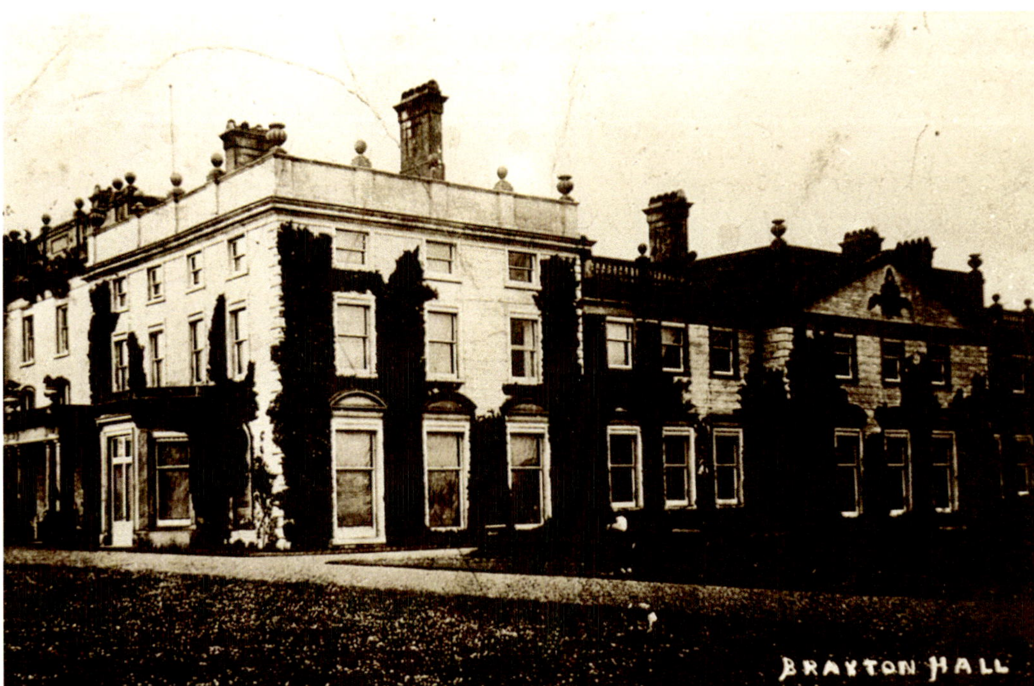


Brayton Hall.

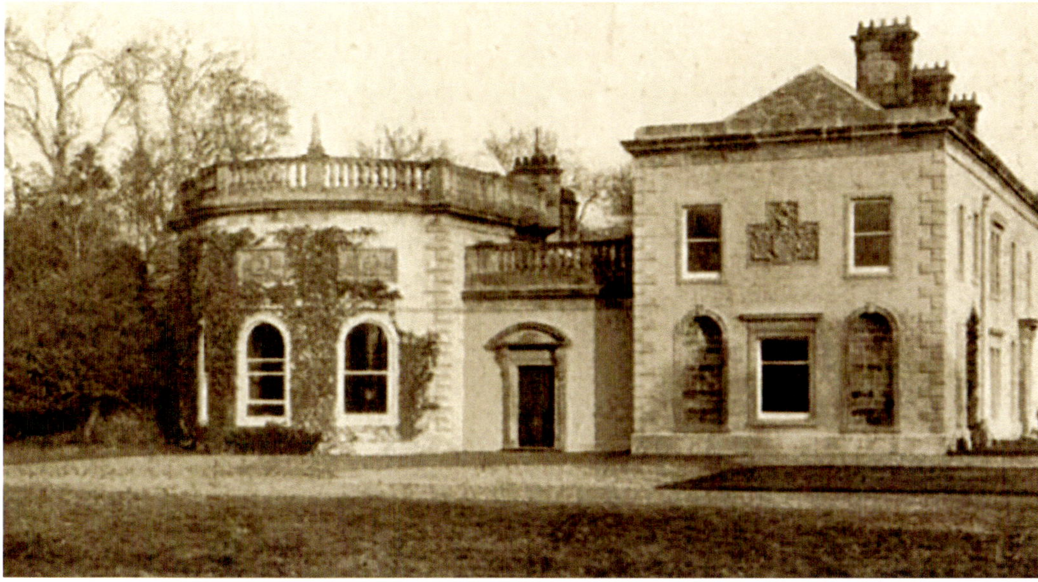

The smaller house of Brayton Hall after the fire.

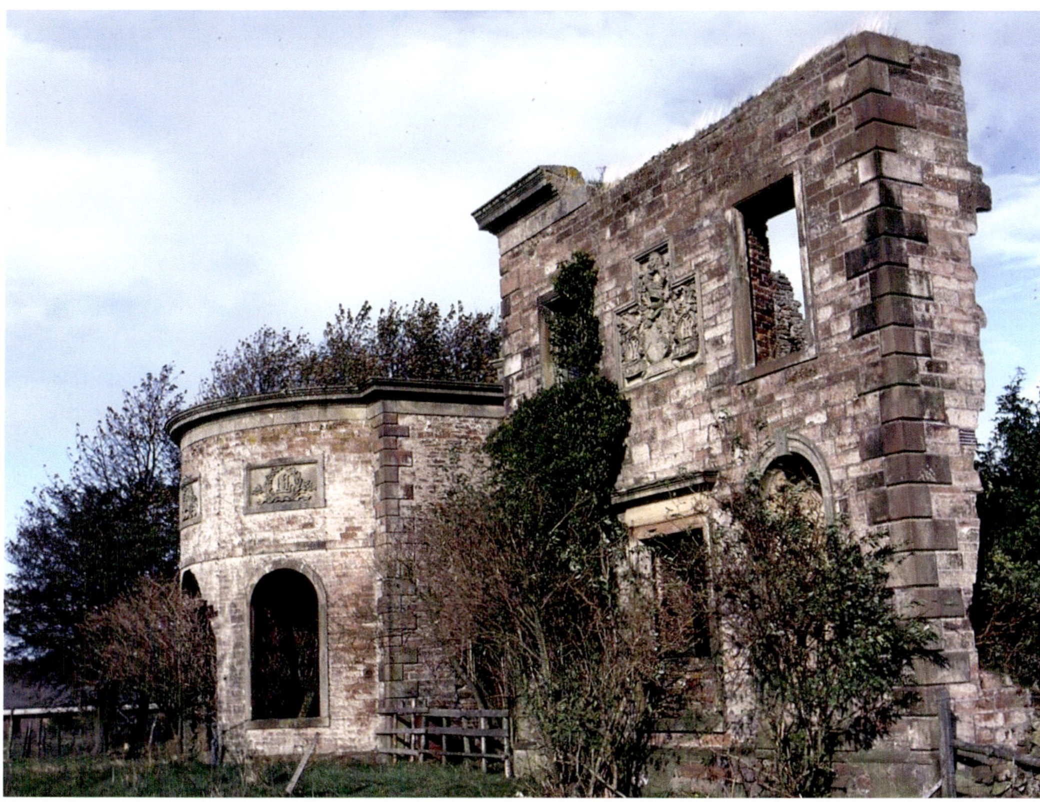

Brayton Hall ruins.

## Bridekirk, Bridekirk

Bridekirk was once the seat of the Young-Thompson family. New houses have been built on its site. The outbuildings survive and have been converted to residential use.

## Bryerswood, Far Sawrey

Joseph Ridgway Bridson built the 'Jacobethan' Bryerswood in 1888 in half-timbered style to the designs of R. Knill Freeman of Bolton, where Bridson's brother was mayor. That there was no tradition of half-timbered building in the area was ignored. Bryerswood contained stained glass by Shrigley and Hunt. The Bridsons acquired Water Park, Greenodd by marriage and made it their seat, selling Bryerswood to the Edmondsons of Wigan who built a model farm for their children, now known as Clock House. The Whittakers followed the Edmondsons and the Naylors bought the house in 1936.

The garden, of which elements including the kitchen garden and greenhouses remain, was Thomas Mawson's first commission. Bryerswood lasted little more than sixty years before being demolished in 1956. The outbuildings of Bryerswood have been converted into a house.

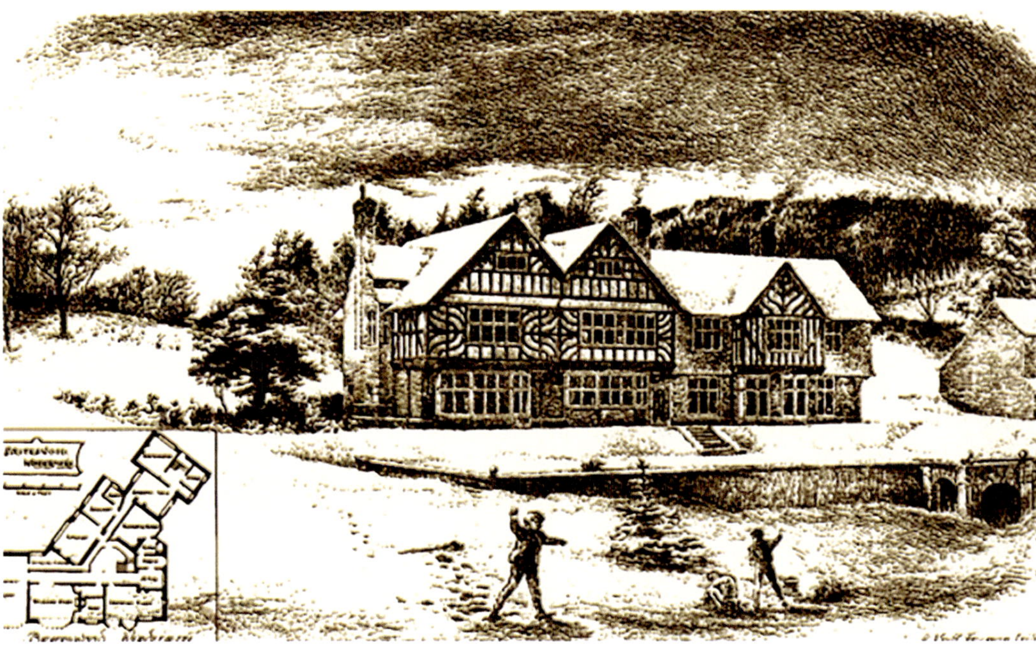

Bryerswood.

## Brougham Hall, Penrith

Little more than the surrounding walls of Brougham survive and now provide a home for a variety of craft workshops. The castle was the ancient fortified seat of the de Burghams, who were probably landowners before the Conquest, but retained their estate under William I. In the late thirteenth century, the estate was

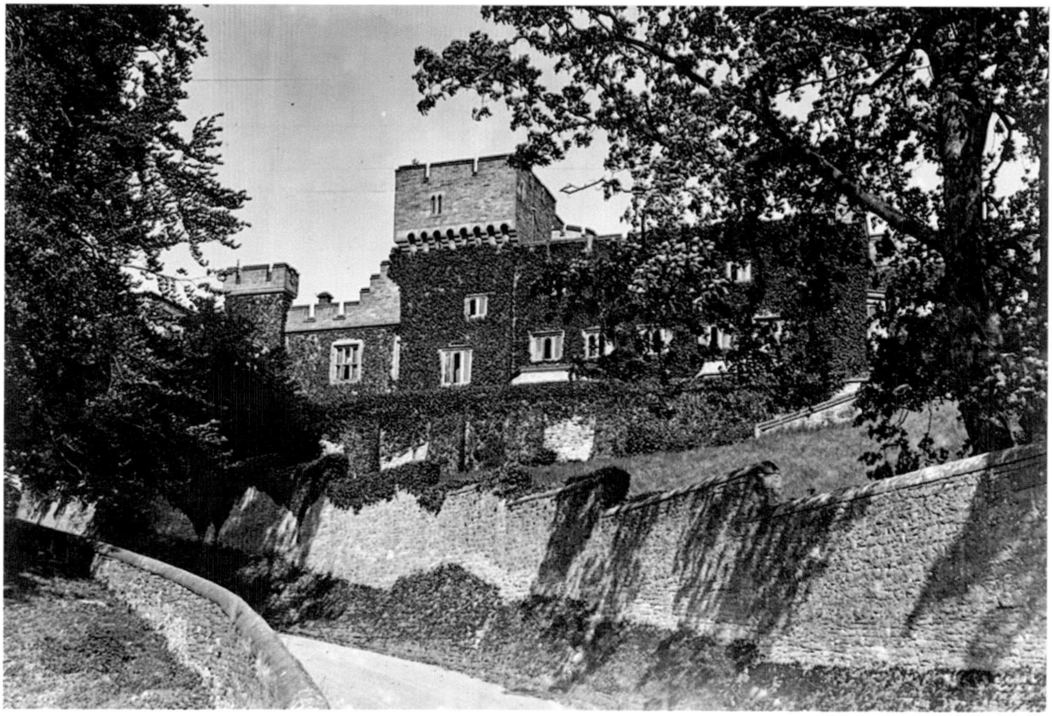

Brougham Hall.

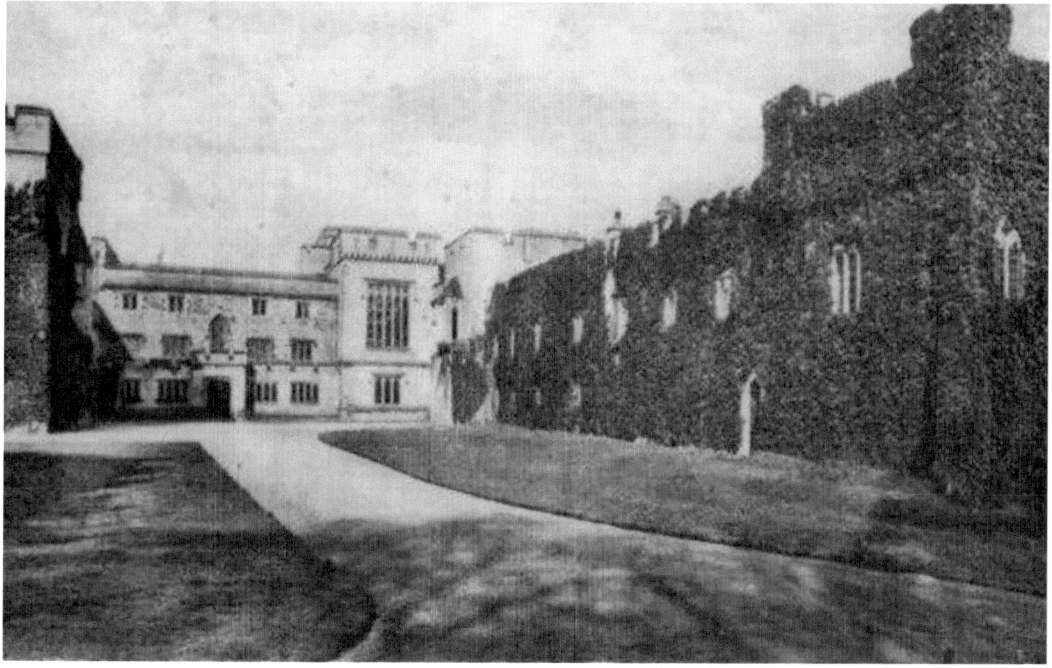

Brougham Hall.

divided between female heirs. The Burghams of Brougham Hall became extinct in 1609 and the hall passed through various hands until Lady Anne Clifford bought one third of it in 1654 for £1,500. By the time Brougham was acquired by Lady Anne, the walls enclosed a manor house, presumably a hall with service rooms and solar, and a pele tower. Additions were made in the late fifteenth century and elements of the walls together with gates dating from 1520, survive from this period. Lady Anne Clifford also rebuilt the nearby chapel of St Wilfrid, whose rector in the early twentieth century was Beatrix Potter's brother-in-law; Potter was a regular visitor to the castle. The chapel is now in the care of the Churches Conservation Trust.

After her death, James Bird, Lady Anne's lawyer and steward, who already owned two thirds of the property, bought her third, becoming the first person to hold the entirety of the estate for almost 300 years. Bird moved the villagers from near the hall to Eamont Bridge, creating for himself an extensive deer park, building the surviving gatehouse and constructing a house within the castle walls known as Hill House. After James Bird died, his son-in-law Thomas Carleton sold the hall and its estate to John Brougham of Scales Hall in 1726 for £5,000. John, who belonged to a different branch of the de Brougham family, had grown wealthy as an excise commissioner.

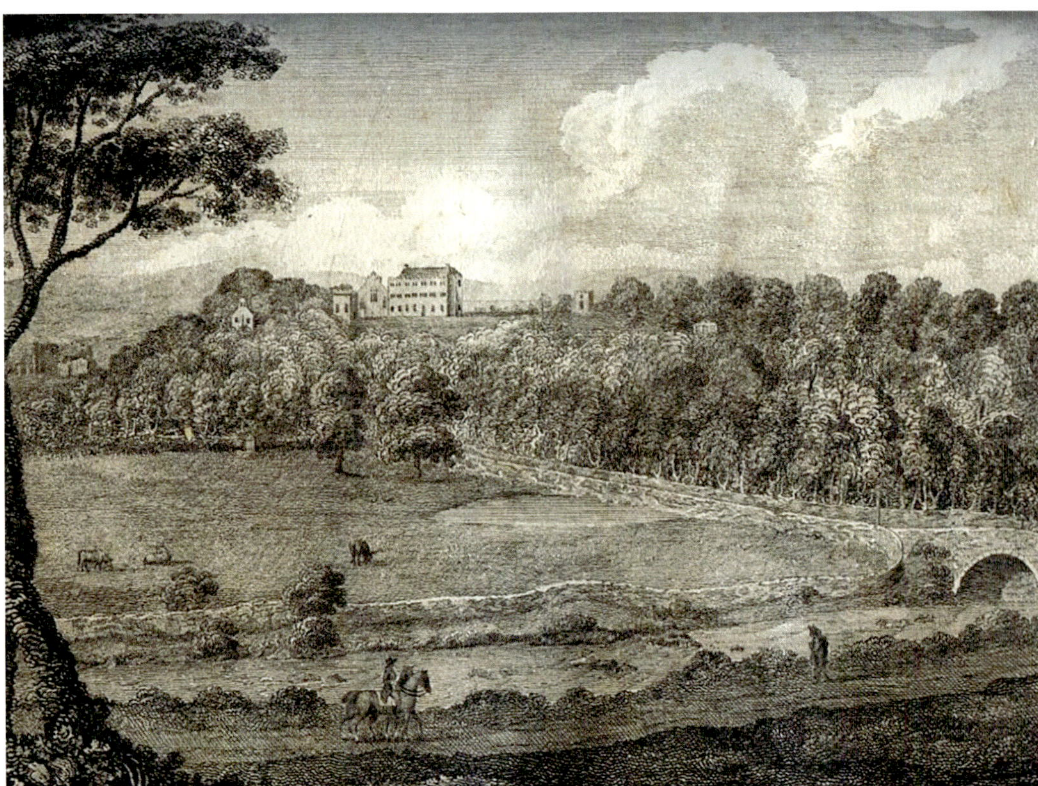

Brougham Castle showing James Bird's house of 1680.

In the nineteenth century, Brougham Hall became known as 'the Windsor of the North', admittedly on a much smaller scale, and was visited by King Edward VII, the future King George VI and other members of the royal family, as well as superior persons such as Lord Curzon. At its height, the estate covered more than 5,000 acres and the hall had seventy indoor staff.

John Brougham was succeeded by his nephew, whose son Henry was the father of Henry Peter, 1st Baron Brougham and Vaux, Lord Chancellor of England, fellow of the Royal Society and inventor of the eponymous carriage. Henry Brougham largely neglected his estates, the castle becoming known by locals as 'the Birds' Nest', its chapel used as a barn. Henry Peter inherited the estate in 1810, having begun his distinguished, if distinctly dramatic, political career the same year as MP for Camelford. He qualified at the English and Scottish Bars, helped found the *Edinburgh Review* and in 1820 became Attorney General to Queen Caroline, having defended her against the Prince Regent's attempts to divorce her. An acknowledged radical, he would later work to abolish the slave trade, reform the judicial system and do away with rotten boroughs – the latter is rather ironic given his inability to hang onto any particular seat for long and his reliance on winning pocket and rotten seats himself. In 1828, he made a six-hour speech, the longest ever made in the House of Commons and in 1830 he was appointed Lord Chancellor and made 1st Baron Brougham and Vaux. As both a journalist and an advocate, he had a talent for making enemies, including Lord Byron (a great hater), who wrote of him:

> too much of a lawyer for the people – and too much of a demagogue for Parliament-[...] representative at last upon sufferance of the proprietor of some rotten borough, [....] and the outcast of all parties – his support has become alike formidable to all his enemies – (for he has no friends) and his vote can be only valuable when accompanied by his silence.

A modern authority describes him as 'unpopular, indiscreet and devious'. He was a fully paid-up member of the awkward squad with the money to indulge himself. In 1832, radical as ever, he was instrumental in forcing the Great Reform Bill through Parliament. Brougham never again held office after 1834, devoting the remainder of his life to education, the law and founding Cannes, where he was buried and a statue of him stands on the waterfront. His two daughters predeceased him and he was succeeded in his peerages, according to a special remainder, by his younger brother William, omitting a swathe of closer male heirs.

In 1829 part of Brougham Hall had collapsed and Brougham had decided to rebuild virtually the entire hall, retaining little more than the defences of the older building. Between 1820 and 1843 L. N. Cottingham (and later his son) were therefore retained to restore Brougham Hall and build a large irregular mansion within the walls of his ancestral home. As part of these developments, the medieval hall, said to be the largest in Cumbria and measuring more than 100 feet by 35 feet, was swept away and the pele tower heightened to contain a water tank. As late as 1863, a library and octagonal vaulted billiard room were completed

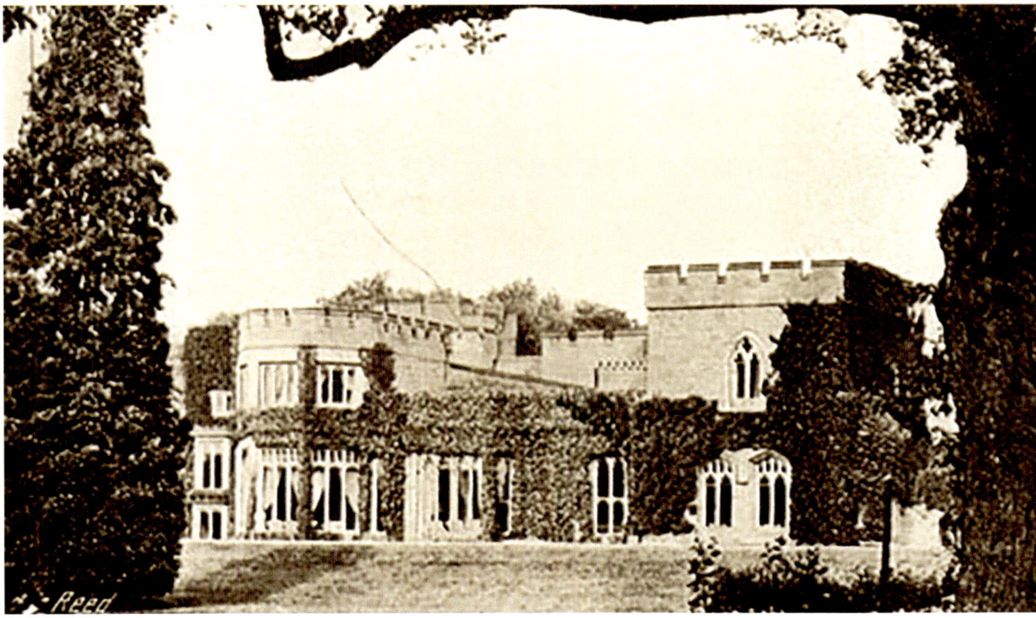


Brougham Hall.

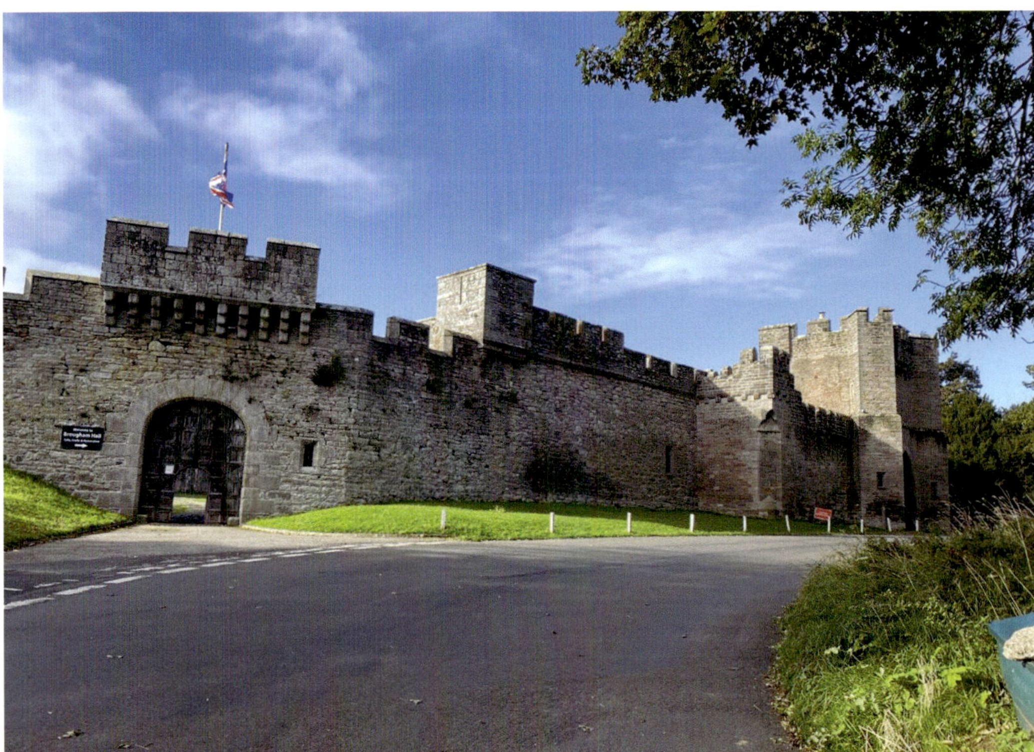

Brougham Hall.

to the designs of Richard Charles Hussey. Although the house had thirty-nine bedrooms, there was only one bathroom.

The residential range was essentially L shaped with service rooms around a courtyard behind the right-hand wing and the Lord Chancellor's vaulted study at the extreme left. It is difficult now to imagine the castle at its nineteenth-century zenith due to the extensive demolition and very close encroachment by modern housing. Nothing remains of the once impressive gardens.

None of the later barons had Henry Peter's talents and the financial incontinence of the feckless 4th Baron Brougham, not helped by his decision to become a professional gambler in an attempt to save his estate, led to the hall being sold to settle debts in 1934. It was bought by Geoffrey Carleton Cooper but was soon stripped of its contents and the mansion largely demolished, leaving only some service rooms and the outer walls. During the Second World War, Brougham Hall was used as a secret tank base by the Royal Armoured Corps and housed Polish refugees. In 1967 it was bought by a local builder with proposals for a caravan site, trades union centre and motel.

Fortunately, the same year, Christopher Terry acquired what remained of Brougham Castle and began its stabilisation and restoration. Unfortunately, he was unable to stop insensitive and inappropriate houses being built by the company which had bought the hall. Brougham Castle now belongs to a charitable trust and is open to the public. Fragments of the castle can be found in a number of local buildings.

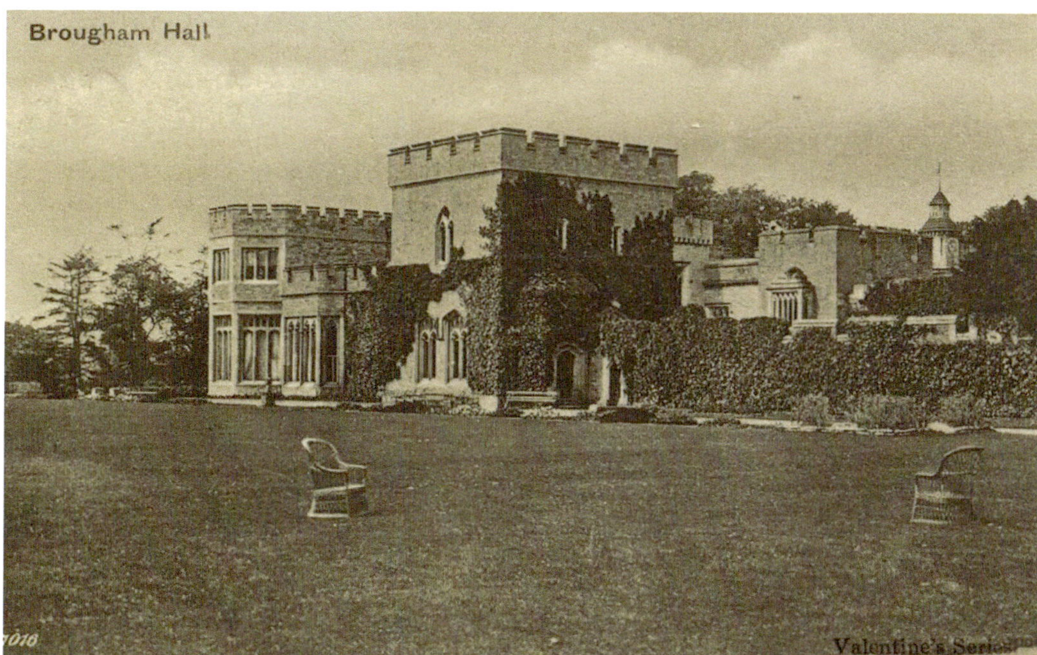


Brougham Hall. The terrace was artificial, created by banking up soil and held in place by buttresses.

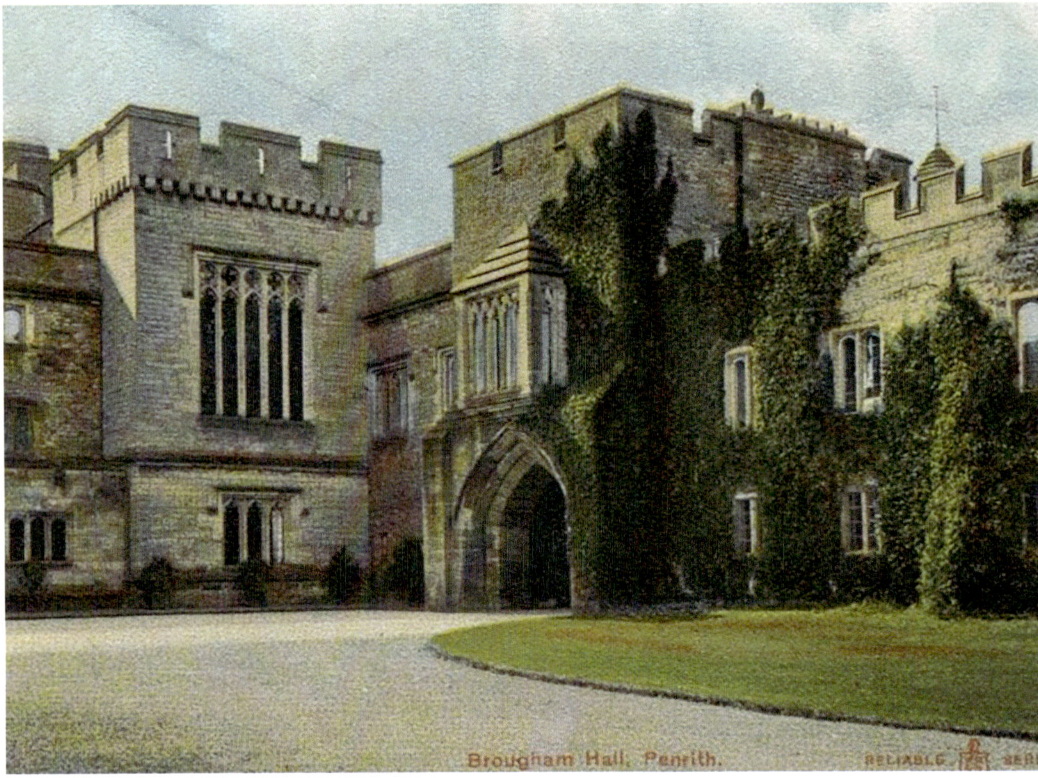


Brougham Hall.

## Cleator Hall, Cleator

After 1776 when Wilson Gale succeeded to the Bradyll estates, Cleator became the seat of the tobacco trading Gale family of Whitehaven, who were amongst the richest of the west coast merchants in the seventeenth and eighteenth centuries. Cleator Hall was sold in 1842 after the Gale-Bradyll family fortunes declined as a result of extravagant spending at Conishead Priory, another of their homes. Mildred Gale, who died in Whitehaven in 1701, was the grandmother of George Washington, first president of the United States. Cleator Hall was later the seat of the Lindows, who became rich from local iron ore and limestone and were prominent in local society.

## Cockermouth (Old) Hall, Cockermouth

Built in the reign of Elizabeth I, Cockermouth Hall was the original seat of the Fletchers, whose descendants are still seated at Hutton-in-the-Forest, which they acquired in 1606, after which Cockermouth Hall became a dower house. Mary Queen of Scots is said to have stayed for three nights at the hall under the hospitality of Henry Fletcher on her journey from Workington to Carlisle in 1568. According to legend he entertained her with great magnificence and gave her robes of velvet. Sir Frederick Fletcher Vane sold Cockermouth Hall at the end of the eighteenth century, after which it was converted into tenements. Following a

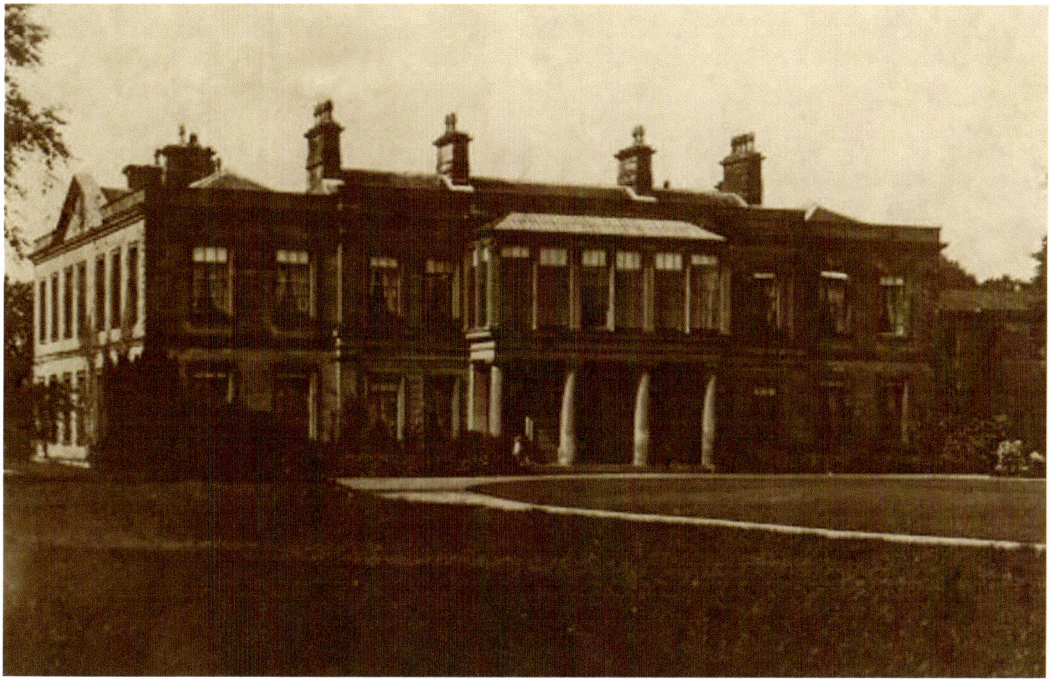

Crofton Hall.

period as a ruin, the hall was demolished around 1970. Stone from Cockermouth Hall is said to have been used in the building of a new house in Papcastle, a Cockermouth suburb.

## Crofton Hall, Thursby

In the thirteenth and fourteenth centuries Crofton was held by the de Crofton family, from whom it passed by marriage to the Brisco family. It remained the seat of the Briscos, prominent on local and national affairs, until it was sold in the early twentieth century after a period of decay.

After his defeat at the Battle of Hexham in 1464, King Henry VI sought safety at Crofton Hall before moving on to Crackenthorpe Hall, where the lord of Crofton's sister Margaret Brisco was lady of the manor and Henry disguised himself as a gardener to avoid capture. When a Scots army led by James V of Scotland invaded England in 1542, Sir Robert Brisco led the English army at the Battle of Solway Moss. The site of the battle includes a mound known as Brisco Hill, marking the site where Sir Robert was killed leading a cavalry charge. Colonel William Brisco was a fanatical Parliamentarian and witchfinder who narrowly escaped being a regicide due to his carefully timed absence on his estates at the time of the trial of Charles I.

Sir John Brisco was made baronet of Crofton in 1782. He carried out major improvements to the estate, including adding a deer park and planting forestry. Through his marriage to Lady Carolina Fleming – who was painted by Thomas

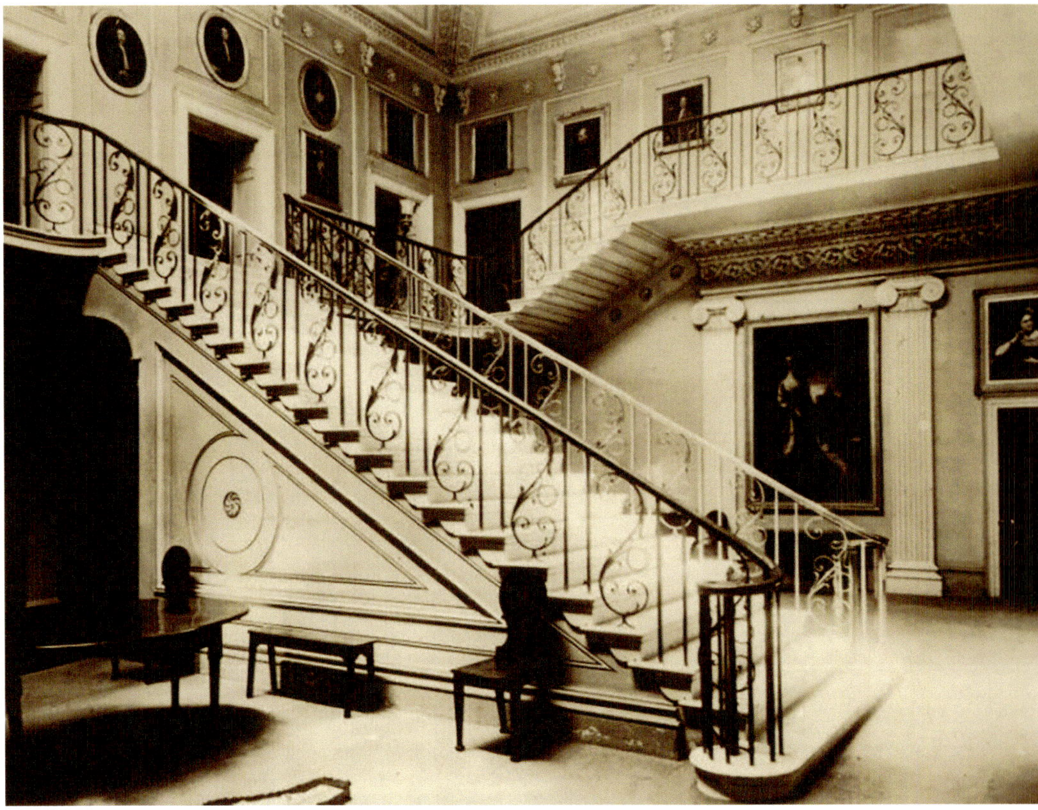

The staircase hall, Crofton.

Gainsborough the year they wed and the portrait hung at Crofton Hall – Sir John inherited two plantations on present-day St Kitts. He was succeeded by his son Sir Wastell in 1805. Escaping nominative determinism by the skin of his teeth, he dragged his wife Sarah into various sexual scandals, requiring the intervention of George IV to sort them out (and George certainly knew a thing or two about sexual scandal). Sir Wastell impoverished his family estate, which never really recovered from his excesses.

Despite ongoing financial decline, the Briscos did everything they could to keep up appearances, further worsening their chronic shortage of cash. Their guests at Crofton included the Prince of Wales (later Edward VII) and his brother Prince Arthur, Duke of Connaught. Inevitably circumstances caught up with them and in 1922 Sir Hylton Brisco, 5th Baronet, was reported missing from the P&O liner *Narkunda* en route from Bombay. A subsequent inquest declared him dead and the estate passed to his sister Hilda. In 1936 the property was bought by the Land Settlement Association for use as smallholdings for unemployed local men. The hall was demolished in the late 1950s. Parts of the house dated from 1665, with later additions and modifications in the 1820s. The Ionic archway with flanking lodges (but without the statue of a deer) and stable block survive, as does an octagonal lodge.

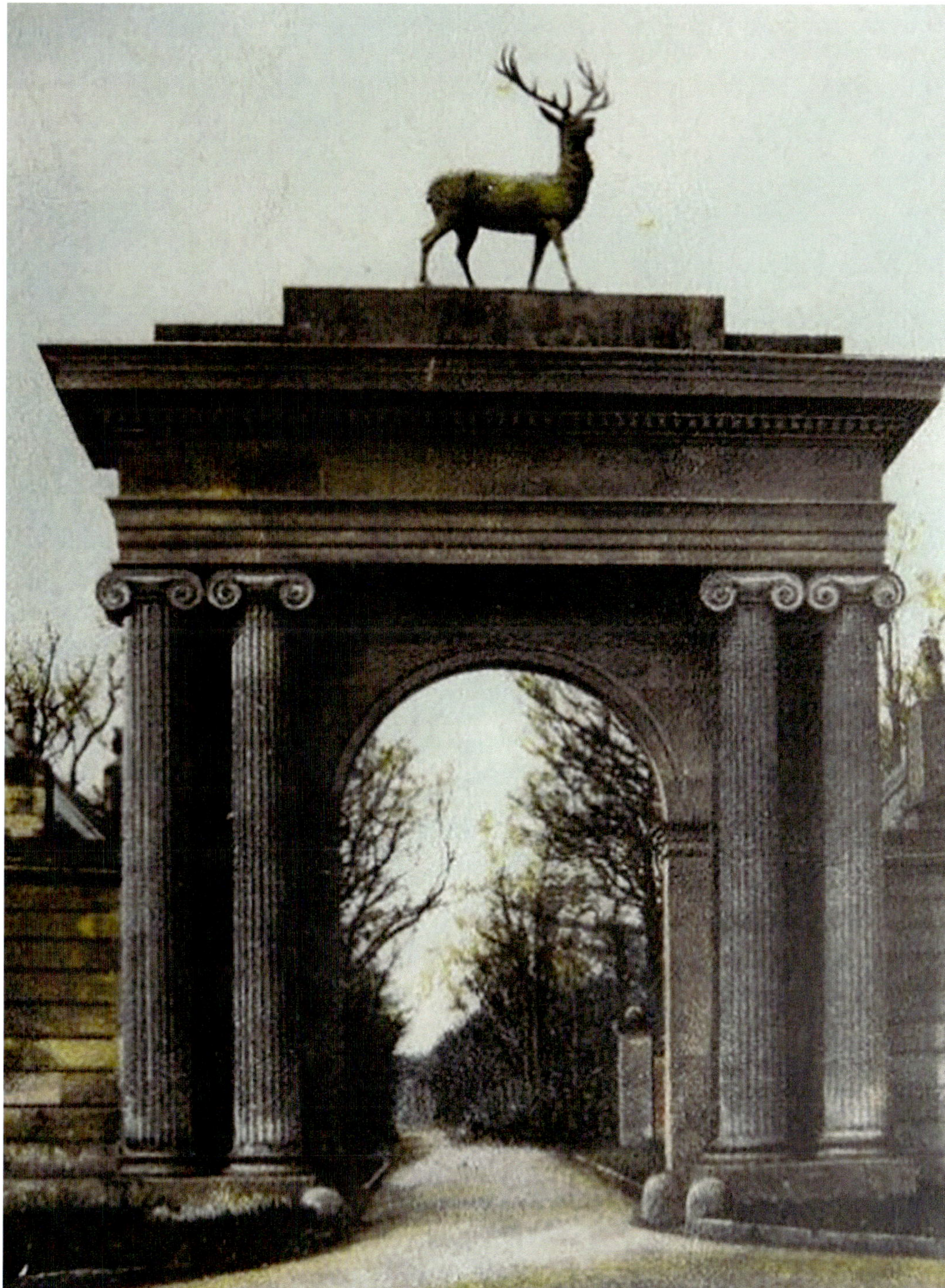

Crofton Hall entrance arch. The arch survives but the stag does not.

## Cunswick Hall, Underbarrow

The present farmhouse at Cunswick dates from the early nineteenth century and stands on the site of an earlier house which was the seat of the Leyburn(e) family from the fourteenth until the eighteenth century and once stood in its own deer park. Fragments of wall and a sixteenth-century window, which is said to contain the oldest glass in Westmorland, survive from the first house. The original gatehouse, dating from the fifteenth or sixteenth century, also survives in a much-altered state with the Tudor royal arms over the arch; a pele tower is said to have been demolished in the 1580s when the clock and bell it contained were given to the people of Kendal.

Roger de Leyburne, heir to Cunswick, murdered his father Sir Charles, claiming his body had been lost in a flood. Sir Charles' body with fatal stab wounds was later found by the river and Roger took his own life, allegedly fulfilling a prophecy that 'one Leyburne would rest uneasy, would whiten the rocks of Cunswick Scar and would haunt the hall'. A later Leybourne refused to swear loyalty to Elizabeth I, describing her as a 'usurper, illegally queen, and a lascivious and very wicked woman'. His words resulted in his execution at Lancaster and the punitive demolition of their defensible pele tower. The Leybournes forfeited what was left of the property to the Crown after the family backed the Jacobites in their failed 1715 rebellion. In 1721 it was sold to Thomas Crowle, whose family owned it until it became part of the Lowther estates in 1753, after which it became a farmhouse and most of the remaining medieval buildings were demolished. Cunswick was sold to the Cropper family in 1920 and they still own it.

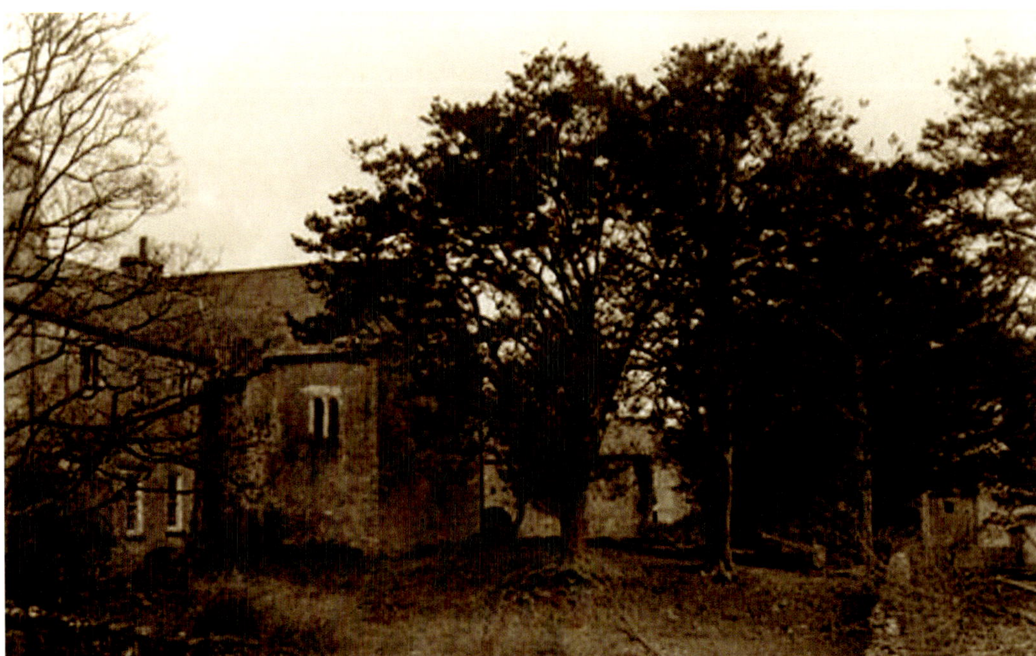

Cunswick Hall.

## Dalton Hall, Dalton

The present Dalton Hall, built in 1968–72 for the Mason-Hornby family, was the final commission of Sir Clough Williams-Ellis, designer of Portmeirion. The Hornbys have owned the estate since the late eighteenth century and Williams-Ellis's new house replaced a much larger Georgian building enlarged in 1859–60 by Edmund Hornby, to the designs of the Lancaster architect Edward Graham Paley. This hall was demolished in 1968. Pevsner described its replacement as 'a stately doll's house'. The main fronts of the new house are symmetrical, each with seven bays and two storeys with a pediment and shallow pilasters. A classical temple in the grounds was constructed by Williams-Ellis from the porch of the old house. The estate remains the seat of the Mason-Hornby family.

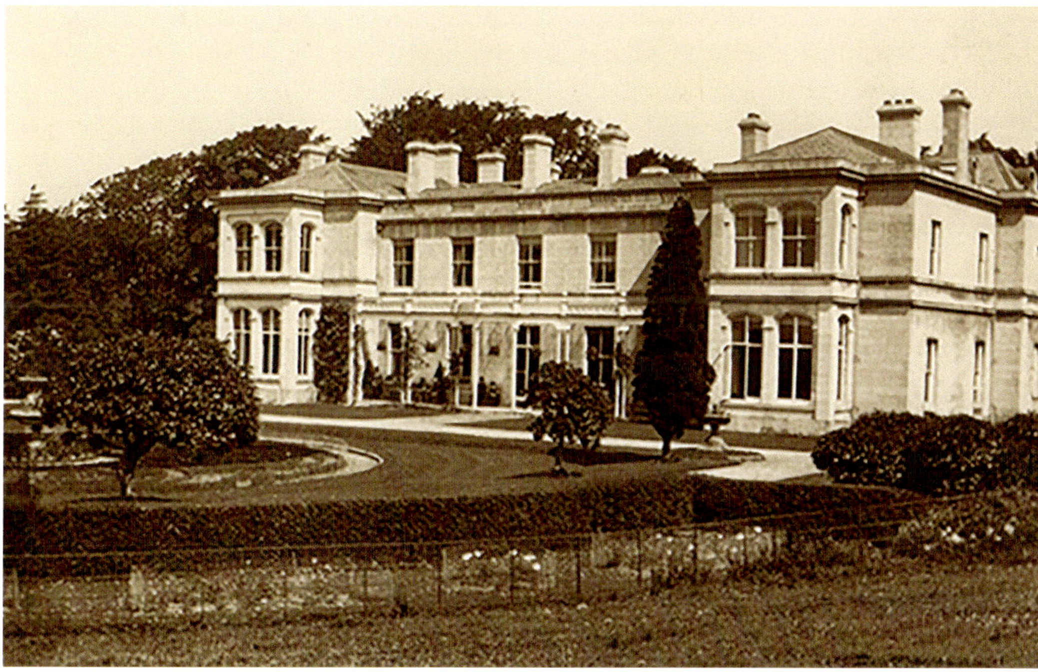

Dalton Hall.

## Distington Hall, Distington

A large undistinguished Victorian house with canted bay windows, Distington was built by local ironmaster Charles Fisher and occupied by the Fisher family until the early twentieth century. A crematorium now stands on the site.

## Eden Hall, Penrith

The Musgraves were one of north-east Cumbria's pre-eminent families from at least the thirteenth century, seated originally at Hartley Castle. After the latter's demolition in 1735 the lead and wooden fittings were used in the construction of their new hall. They were created baronets in 1611. Eden Hall had been granted to Peter de Brus in the twelfth century, was later held by the Turp and Stapleton

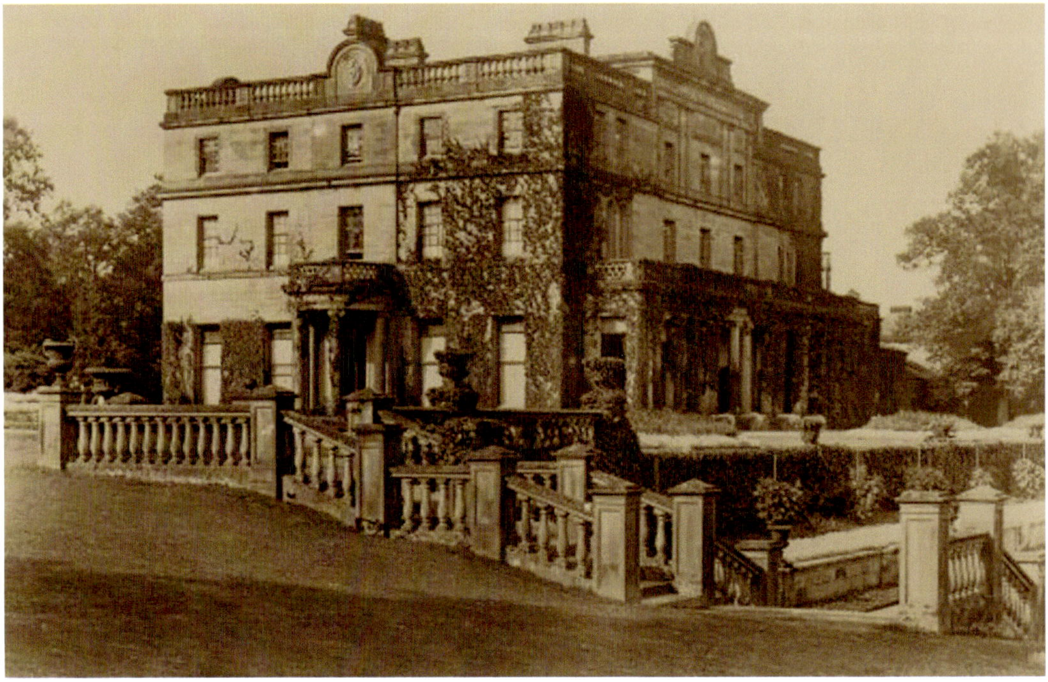

Eden Hall.

families and passed to the Musgraves by the marriage of Joan Stapleton to Thomas Musgrave in the fifteenth century. In 1821 the house was replaced by a new hall designed by Robert Smirke, who worked in a very different style at Lowther Castle. The hall was either rebuilt or remodelled around 1860. In the early twentieth century, faced with mounting death duties, the Musgraves sold Eden Hall and moved to London. The hall was demolished in 1934. The local legend that the hall was dismantled, shipped to America and reconstructed is sadly without foundation. For the past eight decades, the estate has been owned and run by four generations of the Holden-Hindley family.

The stable yard of 1842, probably by George Webster, survives, having been converted for residential use by Michael Bottomley. It has a dramatic domed octagonal clock tower. The west lodge, probably also by Webster, has quadripartite piers and a cruciform lodge with ionic pilasters. The piers carry the badge of the Musgraves, two arms in armour bearing a wreath.

Eden Hall is perhaps most famous for the 'Luck of Edenhall', which has featured in an opera, manga novel, German romantic ballads, pop songs and the work of Anthony Trollope. According to the legend, the Eden Hall butler was collecting water from St Cuthbert's well near the hall, when he surprised a group of dancing fairies from whom he seized the 'Luck' and refused to give it back. This prompted the fairies to issue the warning: 'If this glass should break or fall, farewell the luck of Edenhall'. Family tradition had it that, tempting fate, the notorious rake the Duke of Wharton would throw the cup across a room for a servant to catch. Although the 'Luck' is intact and in the Victoria and Albert Museum, the

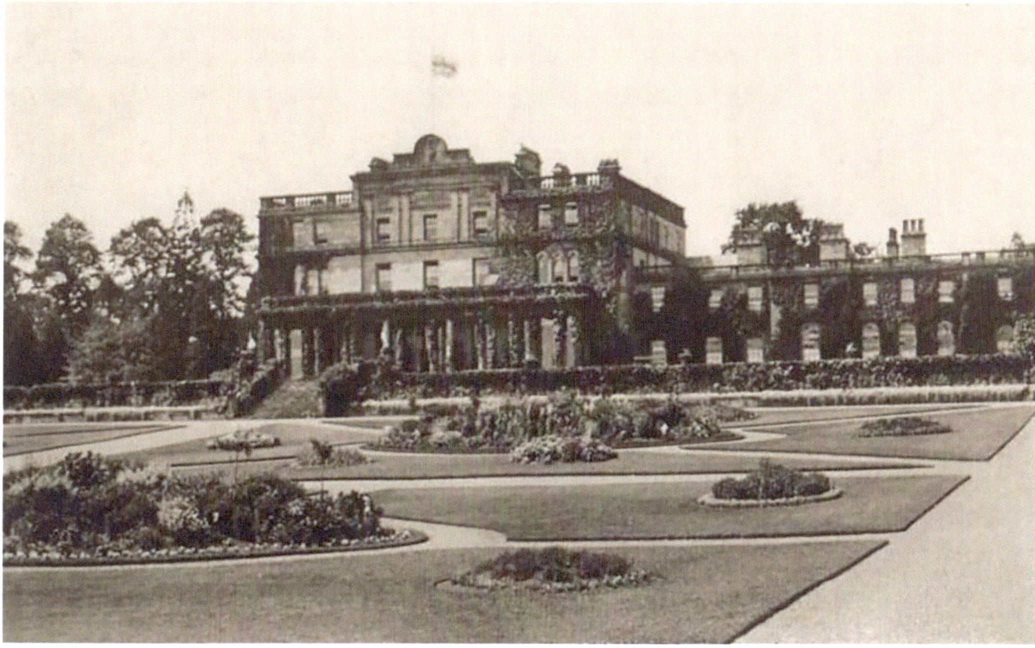

The garden front of Eden Hall.

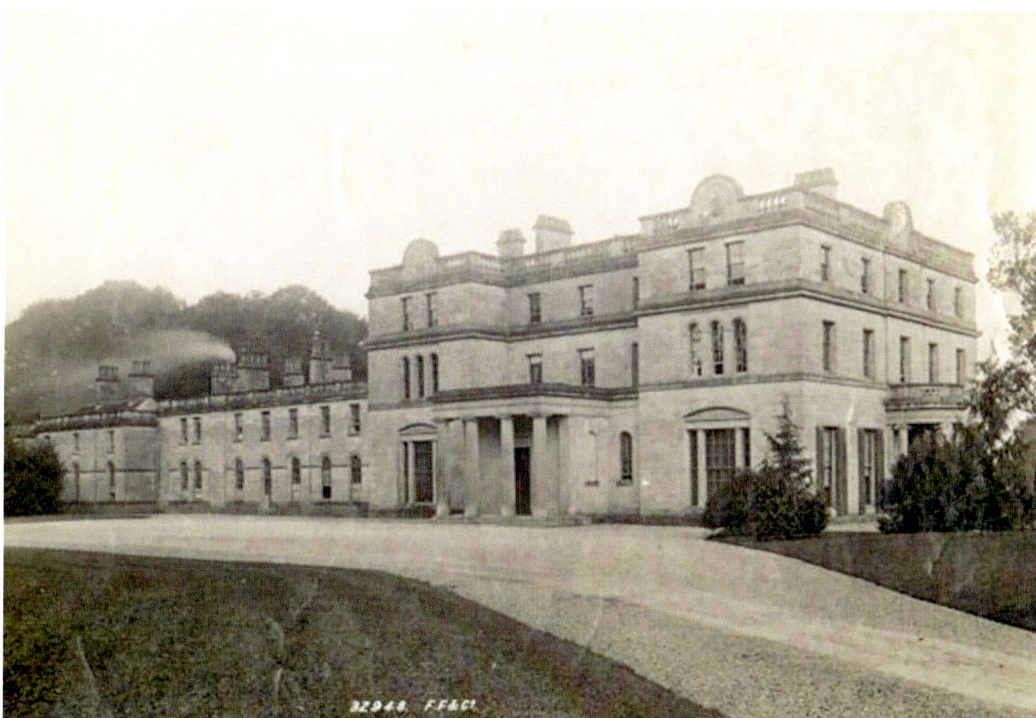

The entrance front of Eden Hall.

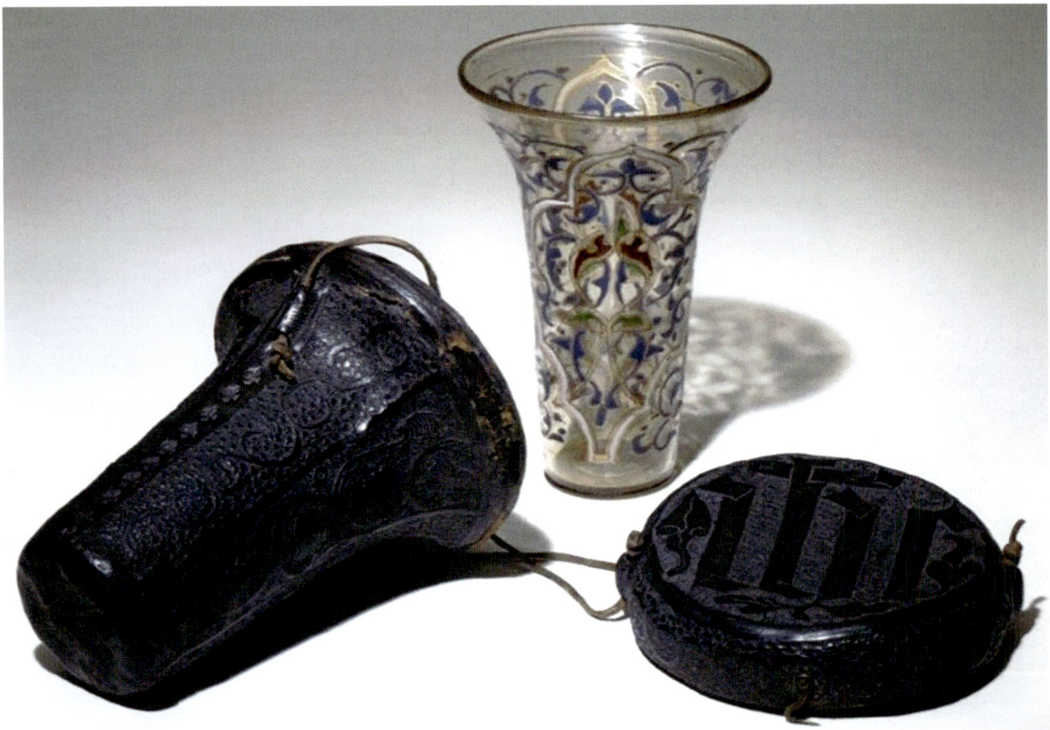

The Luck of Edenhall.

house of Musgrave has indeed fallen. The 'luck' is now recognised as a piece of fourteenth-century enamelled and gilded Syrian glass, which is provided with its own medieval case. The date of its arrival in Britain is unknown but it probably came to the family in the sixteenth century. It is mentioned in the will of Sir Phillip Musgrave in 1677 and was drawn by the famous antiquarian Thomas Machell in 1666.

The Eden Hall 'Luck' is by no means unique in Cumbria: the Luck of Muncaster is a glass bowl kept at the castle and given by Henry VI to Sir John Pennington. Workington Hall was once home to the Luck of Workington, an agate vessel given to the Curwens by Mary Queen of Scots; its departure from Workington with the Curwens is said to have brought ill luck to the town. The Workington 'Luck' was sold by descendants of the Curwens at Sotheby's in 2022. The Luck of Burrell Green is a brass charger associated with the Burrell family and the Luck of Skirsgill is a glass goblet associated with the Whelpdale family.

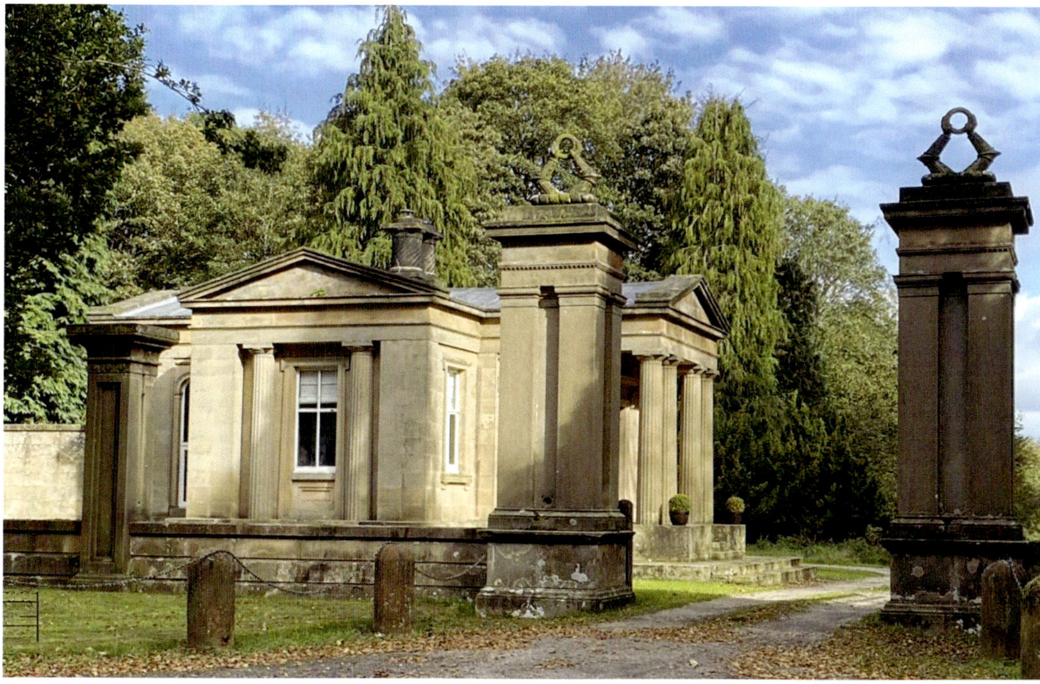

Eden Hall lodge.

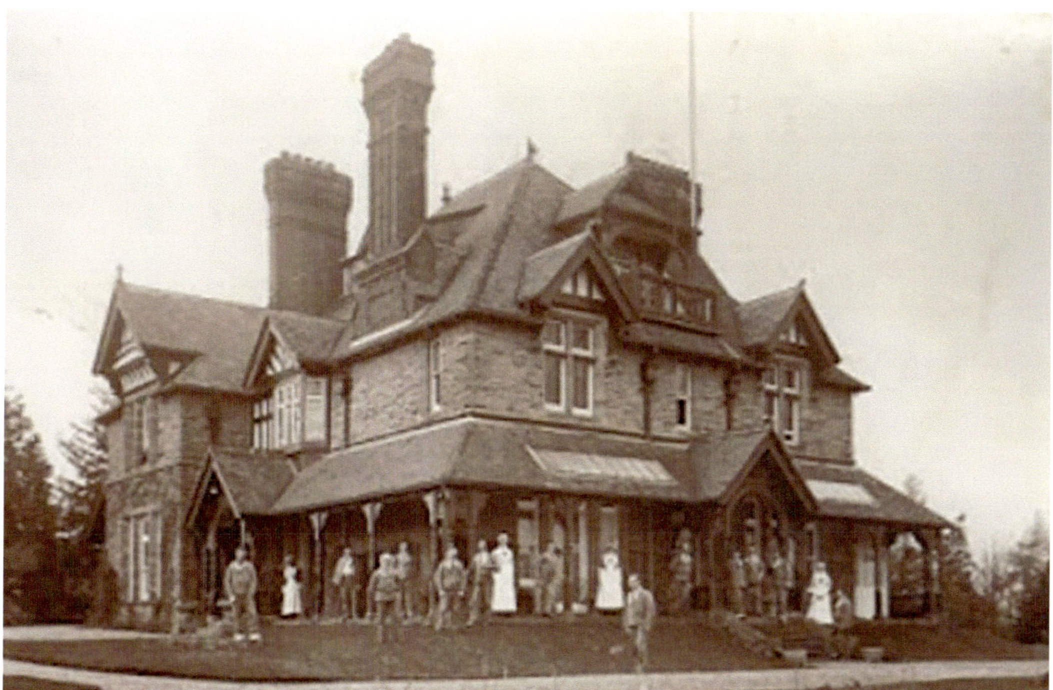

Englethwaite Hall.

## Englethwaite Hall, Armathwaite

Englethwaite was built between 1880 and 1882 by George Henry Hunt for John Tomlinson, who made his fortune as the owner of local gypsum mines in Wetheral. Tomlinson's extravagant living bankrupted him in the 1890s and the hall was subsequently in institutional use: as a school from 1901; as a Red Cross Hospital during the First World War, opening in 1916 with fifty beds and closing in April 1919; and later as a TB sanatorium – the Englethwaite Industrial Colony for Tuberculosis – until 1925. Finally, it was a boys' home from 1933 until 1965. Englethwaite was demolished in 1969 and the site became a caravan park.

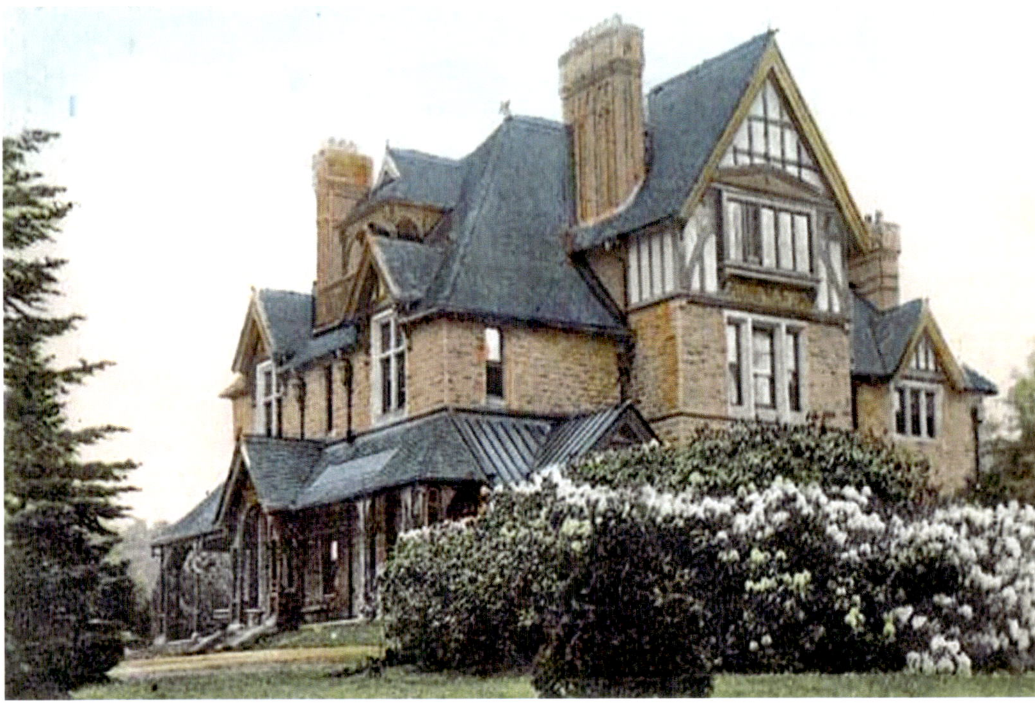

Englethwaite Hall.

## Ewanrigg Hall, Maryport

Ewanrigg, the seat of the Christian family, enjoyed a curious double life: first as a dramatic country house and then, after it was greatly reduced in size, as a rather ramshackle farmhouse, itself destroyed by fire in 2015. The inventory of Anthony Thwaythes of Unerigg in 1585 listed the contents of the Law (Low), Myddle and Heigh (High) towers. When Ewan Christian, of a distinguished Manx family, bought the property, it was reported that he 'hath built a good house out of the shell of an old tower', which suggests the presence of an old pele tower, possibly one of those referred to in Anthony Thwaytes' inventory. Christian is said to have bought Ewanrigg with a small fortune won gambling with the Bishop of Sodor and Man in the late seventeenth century. The Christians married into the best local families, including the Senhouses of Netherhall and the Curwens of Workington. One of Ewan Christian's granddaughters was the mother of the first Lord Ellenborough, who took his title from Ewanrigg's nearby village. HMS *Bounty* mutineer Fletcher Christian was one of Ewan's great-great-grandchildren and the hall was the birthplace of MP and sometime-radical John Christian Curwen.

Ewanrigg was rebuilt around 1750, possibly to the designs of John Addison of Durham, as a striking mansion of seven bays and four storeys, the outer two bays on each side breaking forwards as prominent towers with hipped roofs and plain pediments. There were lower two-storey, three-bay wings to either side, with triple arcades to the ground floors (one of these wings would later become the farmhouse). It is likely that at least one of these towers was originally a pele, although a pele at Ewanrigg is reported to have been built in 1368, rebuilt around 1640 and its ruins completely demolished in 1903. Together these may perhaps represent some or all of Anthony Thwaythes' three towers. Ewanrigg was chosen by Wilkie Collins, who saw it whilst on a walking tour with Charles Dickens, as the model for Limmeridge in *The Woman in White*. Ewanrigg eventually acquired a local reputation for its terrifying apparitions. Its ghosts included the mad widow of Henry Taubmen Christian, its resident for many years, who died in 1859. After Henry's death, the house remained empty and 'no tenant could be found with the temerity to take it'. The estate was put on the market in 1896 on the death of Revd William Bell Christian and in 1897 was sold to J. R. Twentyman, a tea merchant who lived in Shanghai. Twentyman was rarely resident and the house fell into an even greater state of decrepitude, no tenant being found for it.

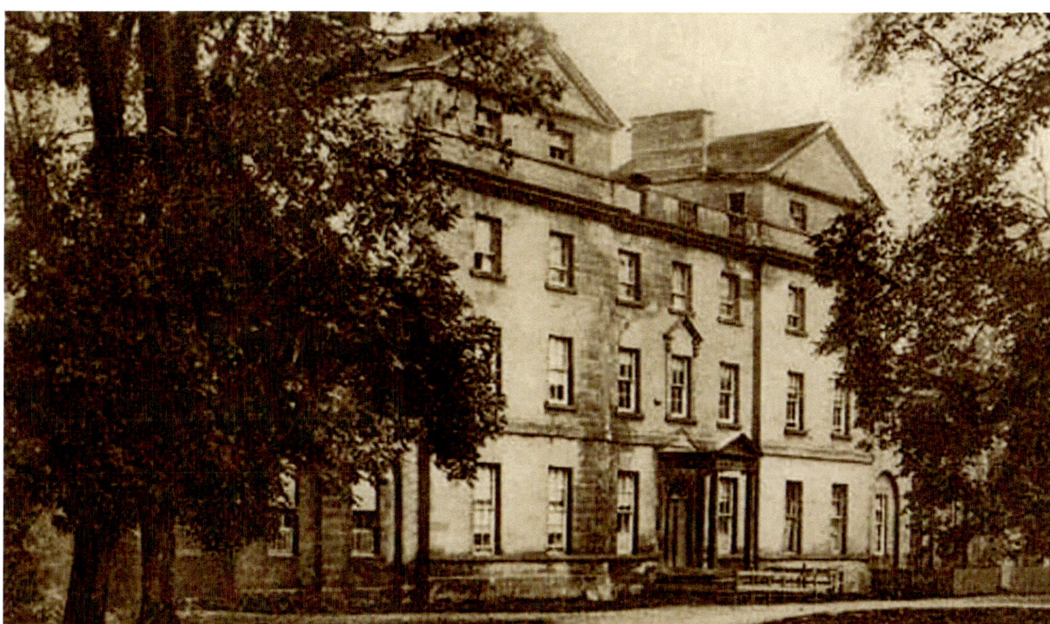

Ewanrigg Hall.

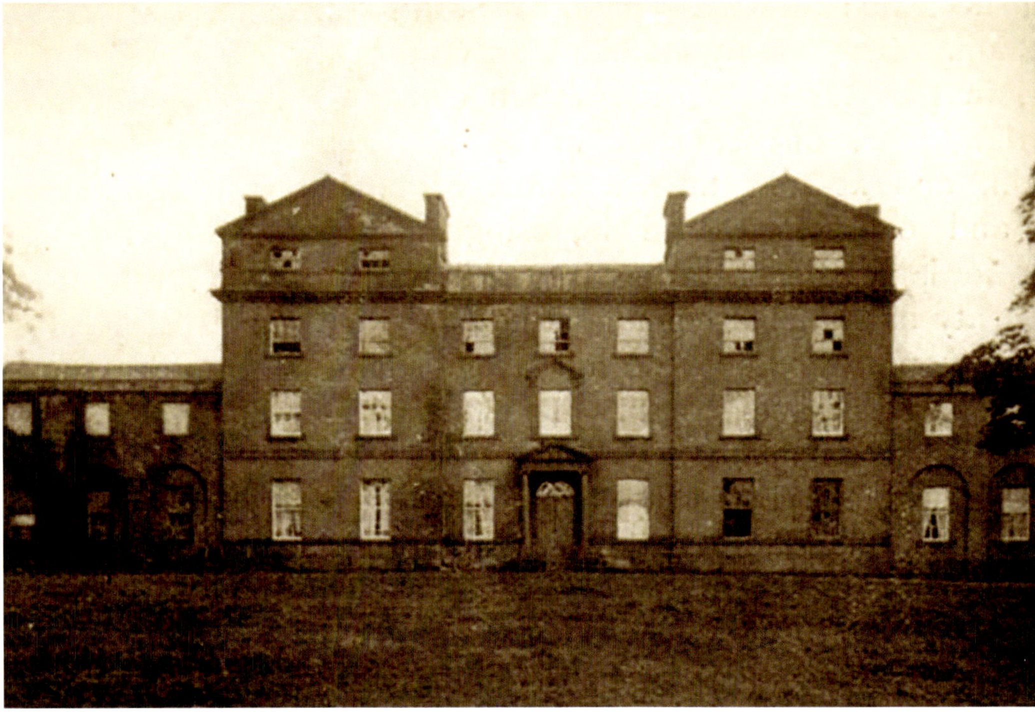

Ewanrigg Hall.

In 1903 Twentyman demolished the top floors of the house, leaving only the ground floor of the central block, and a farmhouse was created in one of the wings. The remains of the hall were sold again some twenty years later. The farmhouse itself fell into decay following the death of its final owner, John Dixon, and its final destruction as a result of a deliberately started fire was perhaps inevitable.

## Fell Foot, Newby Bridge

The southernmost tip of Windermere was used as a crossing point by the monks of Furness Abbey and the land remained entirely agricultural until the discovery of the Lake District as a tourist destination in the eighteenth century. In the 1780s the yeoman farmer owners, the Robinsons, sold their farm to Jeremiah Dixon, merchant and Lord Mayor of Leeds, and his wife Mary, daughter of John Smeaton, builder of the first lighthouse on Eddystone Rock. The Dixons were amongst the first incomers to the Lakes from the northern industrial towns, part of a trickle that would eventually become a flood of industrialists and manufacturers determined to exploit their wealth in enjoying the area's then almost unspoilt tranquillity.

Dixon transformed the farmhouse into a three-storey white stucco villa with glorious views over Lake Windermere. The principal front had a single-storey semicircular bow with Tuscan columns and tripartite windows above. To ensure uninterrupted views Dixon moved a public road from the lake side to the landward side of his new mansion, creating a new and improved landscape around his new home.

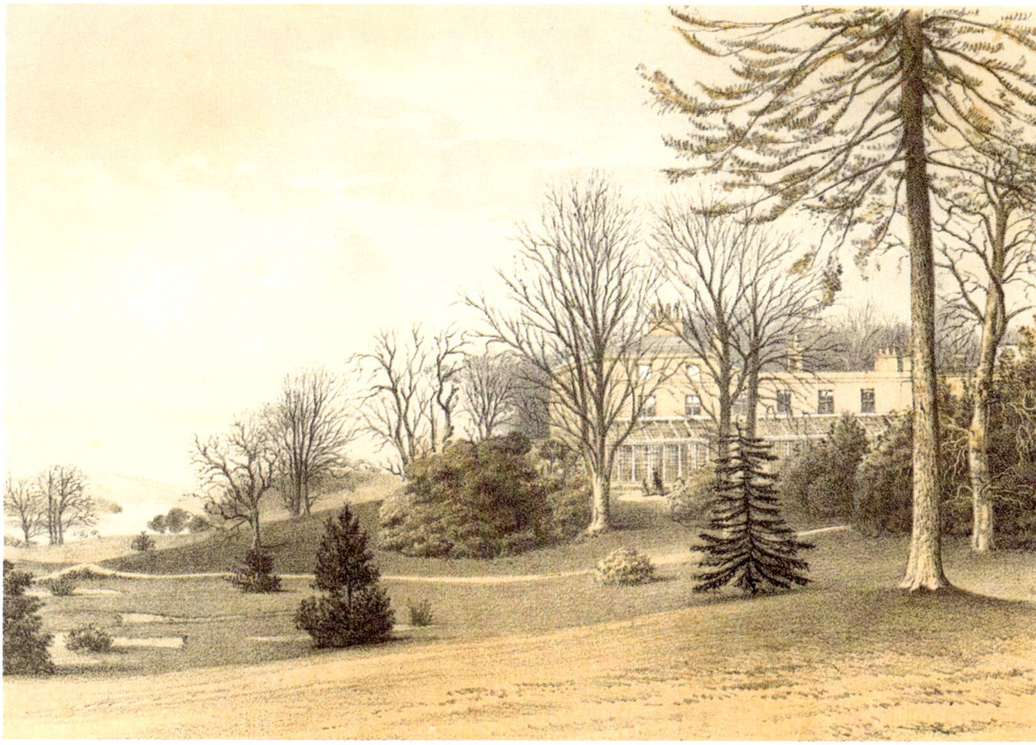

Fell Foot House.

The Dixons sold Fell Foot in 1813 to Francis Dukinfield Astley, a Manchester pit owner. Known as Squire Astley, he was a noted student of forestry, publishing *The Planter's Guide* in 1814. He also hunted his own pack of harriers and published romantic poetry, and used Fell Foot as a summer home. After Astley's death in 1825 the house passed to his infant son of the same name, who would, as an adult, descend on Fell Foot for the summer with his family and fifteen live-in servants.

In 1859 Fell Foot was sold to Colonel George Ridehalgh, a director of the North Lonsdale Iron and Steel Company and founder of the Royal Windermere Yacht Club. Ridehalgh planted an arboretum on his new estate, built stables and kennels and redesigned the interior of his mansion. The property was lit by gas generated on the estate. In 1907 Colonel Ridehalgh's cousin sold the estate to Oswald Hedley, who demolished the house and began to build a neo-Jacobean mansion, the building of which had scarcely begun before his wife died in 1909. Following this tragedy Hedley largely abandoned Fell Foot. In 1948 Hedley's third wife and widow gave a large part of the estate to the National Trust in memory of her husband; it is now a major tourist amenity. Colonel Ridehalgh's miniature dockyard survives with its castellated boathouses and his gas house is a discovery centre for visitors.

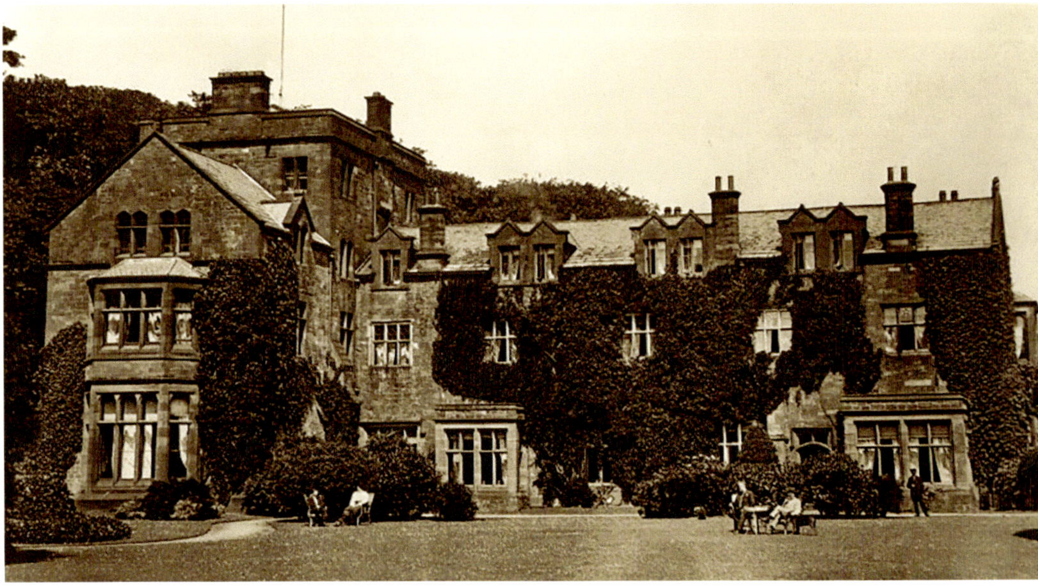

Furness Abbey.

## Furness Abbey, Barrow-in-Furness

At the Dissolution, the mighty Cistercian Furness Abbey was bought by Sir Thomas Curwen, whose son-in-law and successor John Preston built himself a mansion amongst the abbey ruins in the early seventeenth century, probably taking in the guest house of the abbey. The house passed from the Prestons to the Lowthers and then the Cavendishes of Holker Hall, but in 1847 it was bought by the Furness Railway Company, which built a hotel incorporating John Preston's Manor House. The new hotel was intended to accommodate visitors to the abbey, making the most of the newfound convenience of travel by train. The architects were Sharpe and Paley of Lancaster and when first built, despite having thirty-six bedrooms, there were only three bathrooms. The hotel was extended by Edward Paley in 1862, linking it to the newly built Furness Abbey railway station.

The station and the hotel were bombed in 1941, the hotel having been used as the anti-aircraft control centre for the major port and shipbuilding centre at Barrow. As a result of wartime damage, the hotel was largely demolished by the Department of the Environment in 1953 and 1954 in order to reveal the original abbey fabric. The ruins of the abbey were placed in the care of the state by Lord Richard Cavendish in 1923 and are now managed by English Heritage. Part of Paley's design, including the ticket office and refreshment room, which stood on the site of the manor house, survives as the Abbey Tavern. The site of the hotel is now a car park.

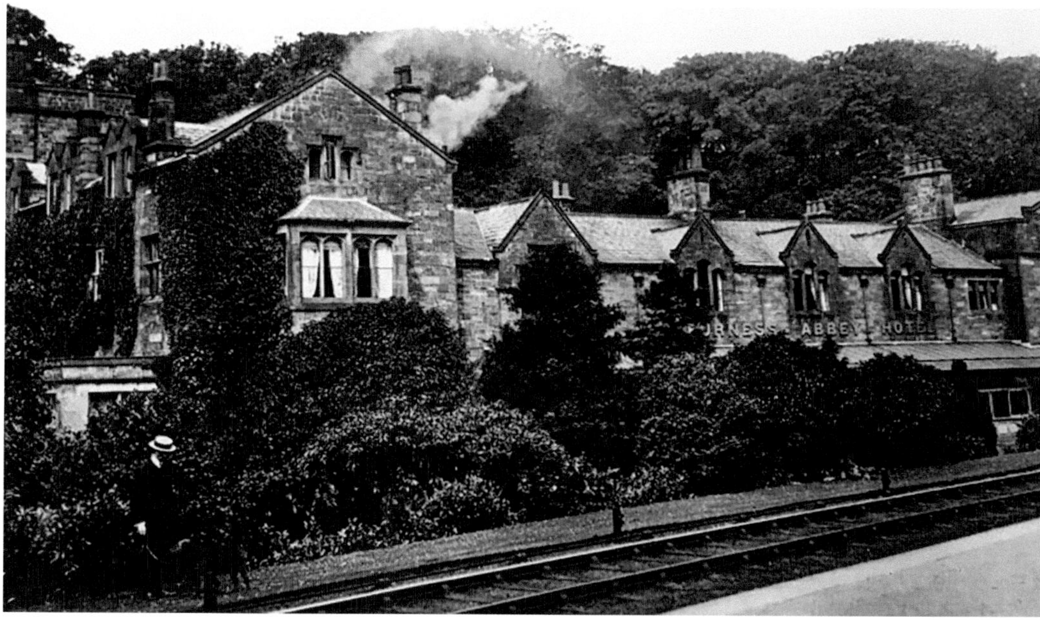


Furness Abbey.

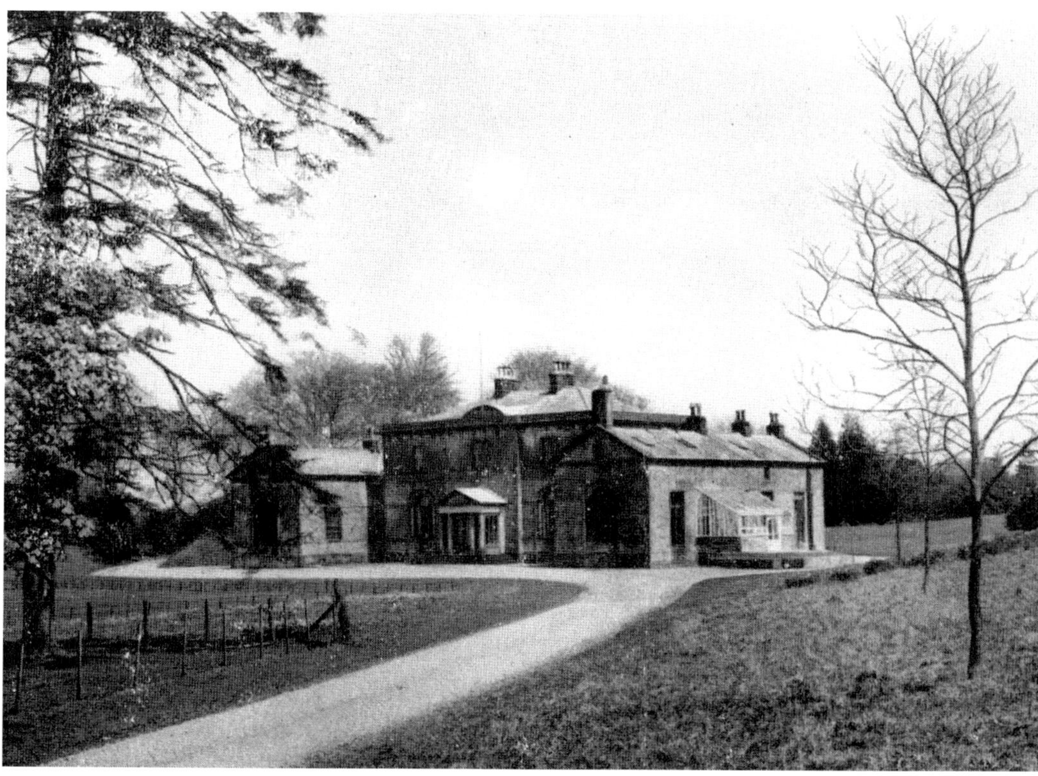

Gilgarron House.

## Gilgarron House, Distington

The Whitehaven merchant William Walker and his sister Anne built Gilgarron between 1805 and 1809. In 1819, William and Anne were abroad buying ornamental trees for their new estate, when the ship in which they were travelling, the *Brunswick*, was attacked by a Spanish gunboat and Walker was killed. The Brunswick reached Italy, but on the return journey Miss Walker, now heiress of Gilgarron, travelled in a British frigate under the command of Captain James Robertson, who had been on board HMS *Victory* at Trafalgar and was described by Rear-Admiral Sir John Marshall as 'a man of transcendent abilities'. Miss Walker and her captain married in Whitehaven in 1825 and the Gilgarron estate remained the seat of their descendants under the name Robertson-Walker for more than a hundred years. On retirement from the Navy, James Robertson-Walker became High Sheriff of Cumberland and the family had a local reputation for philanthropy. In 1940 Mr J Robertson-Walker died and Lt Ian Murdo Maxwell Robertson-Walker was killed serving on HMS *Gloucester* at the Battle of Crete. Double death duties meant that the estate was no longer viable and it was broken up into lots and sold in 1951. The house was demolished and modern housing built on its site after the departure of Mr Austin Robertson-Walker, its last resident.

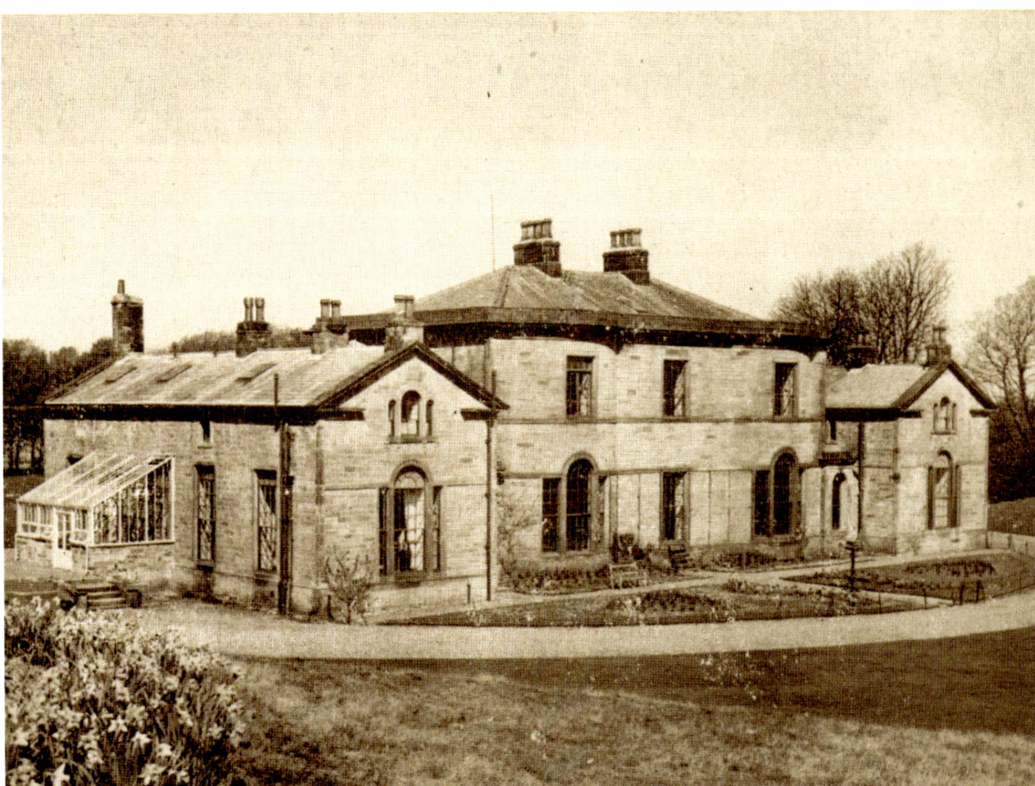

Gilgarron House.

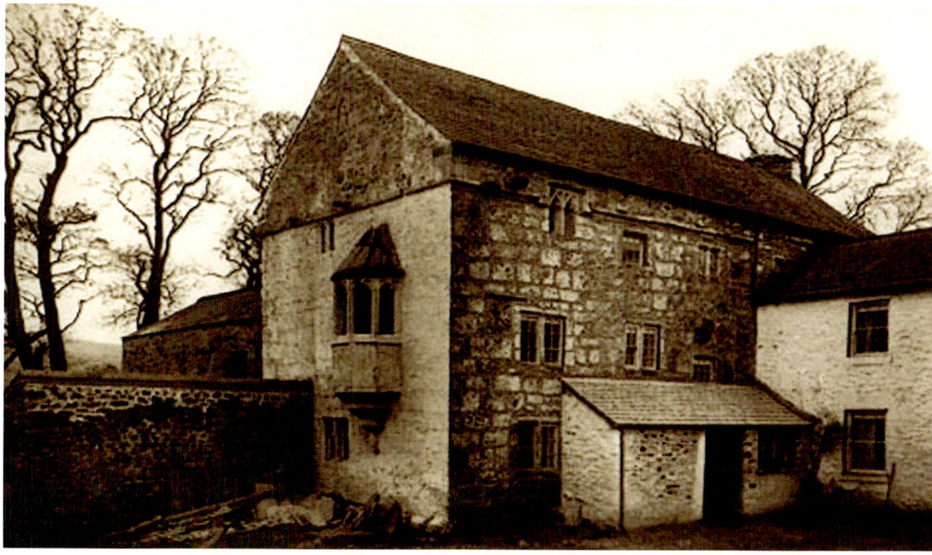

Grange Hall.

## Grange Hall, Asby

Now a farmhouse, and originally a grange of Byland Abbey, only a small part of the fifteenth-century manor house survives, possibly the cross wing of the earlier building. Earlier buildings may have been converted into a pele. The surviving fragment is built of rubble with quoins and a sloped roof was added in the seventeenth century when a turret staircase was also built. An original oriel window survives, suggesting the status of the original building. A carved panel on the first floor has the arms of the Bellingham family, whose seat it once was.

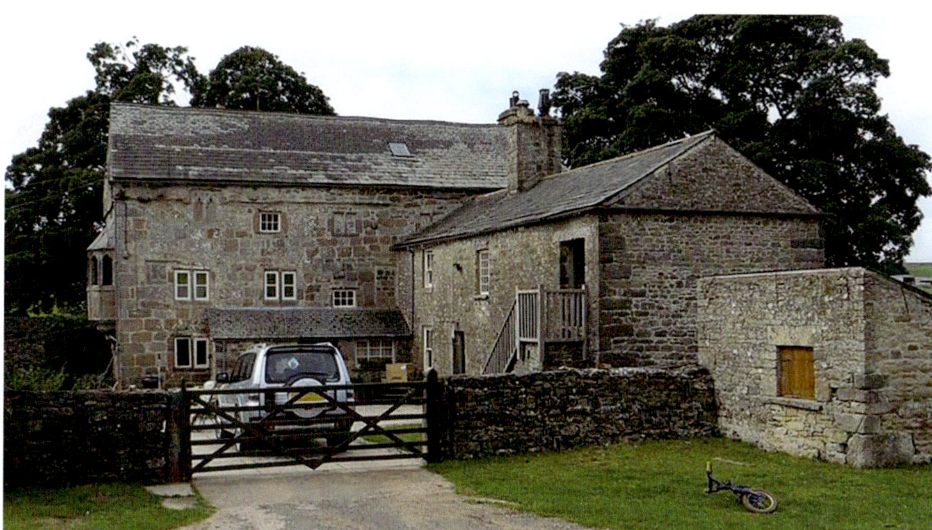

Grange Hall.

## Grimeshill, Middleton

Grimeshill was a seat of the Moore family and originally built in 1690. An advantageous marriage around this time, which carried with it part of the Middleton Hall estate, greatly elevated the status and fortunes of the Moores. One of the house's eighteenth-century inhabitants was Giles Moore, later the rector of Windermere. After his death it was said that Giles, 'by the mere force of genius and application, without the help of an university education, was profoundly learned in history, Latin, Ancient Greek and Hebrew'; he was painted as a young man in 1758 reading the *Iliad*. Grimeshill was almost completely rebuilt to the designs of George Webster in 1836. In 1919 the house was bought by George Morland Beck, a former cattle dealer. The financial slump of the 1930s took its toll on the new owner: Grimeshill was demolished in 1938 and its building materials sold.

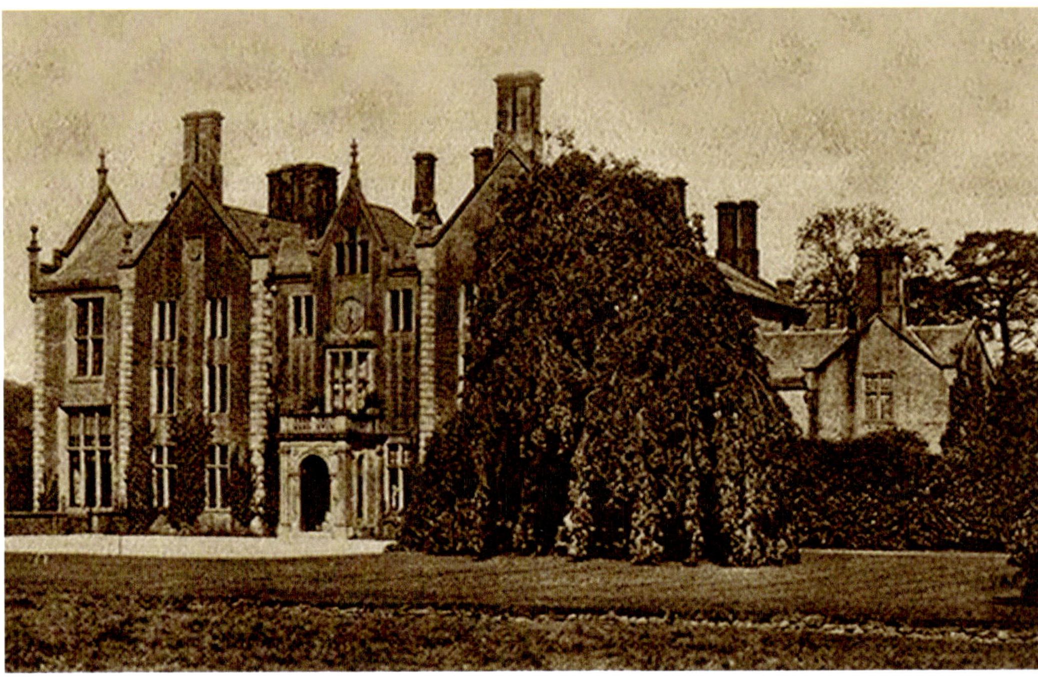

Grimeshill.

## Grizedale Hall, Grizedale

The first Grizedale Hall was built by the Tomlinsons in the thirteenth century. The Rawlinsons married into the Tomlinson family in the early seventeenth century and thus acquired their property at Grizedale. The Rawlinsons grew rich from the proceeds of copper and iron mining and presumably altered or enlarged the house on their new estate. By the eighteenth century the hall had become a farmhouse. Richard Ford acquired part of the estate in the mid-eighteenth century, although apparently not the hall itself. This building was demolished and rebuilt in the early nineteenth century and is now Grizedale Home Farm. Ford built himself a new house in Grizedale known as Ford Lodge, which is said to have been modelled on his previous home in India. Henry Ainslie acquired the estate by marrying Agnes Ford and Montague Ainslie, Richard Ford's great-grandson, who inherited the Grizedale estate in the early nineteenth century, enlarged this house in 1841, creating Grizedale New Hall. The new hall in its turn was pulled down around 1903.

This final Grizedale Hall was built in 1903 for the Liverpool shipowner Harold Brocklebank (see Bolton Hall). Built of slate to the designs of Walker, Carter and Walker of Windermere, the new hall was impressive rather than welcoming. The entrance front, which was more coherent than the garden front, had a prominent tower with a porte-cochere at ground floor level and to its right the windows of the galleried great hall. The garden front was an incoherent mess with terraces, gables, randomly placed bay windows and a colonnade. The main rooms opened off the hall, which had an open roof and chimney piece with carvings of the Four Seasons in Arts and Crafts style.

Grizedale Hall was a private home for only thirty years and was sold to the Forestry Commission in 1936. It was let to the Holiday Fellowship in 1938 for holiday accommodation. During the Second World War it was commandeered by the War Office and became No. 1 POW Camp (Officers), capable of holding around 300 prisoners. The camp was used to hold high-level German prisoners of war including General-Field-Marshal Gerd von Rundstedt. Many of the prisoners were captured U-boat crews, the most notorious of whom was Otto Kretschmer, Germany's most successful submarine commander. As a result, Grizedale was nicknamed 'U Boat Hotel'. An escape attempt in 1940 inspired the 1957 film *The One That Got Away*. The novel *Cage of Eagles* by James Follett was also set at Grizedale. After the war the house was again used by the Forestry Commission, which demolished it in 1957. Parts of the formal garden survive as do the footings of the hall. Grizedale forest is now a sculpture park.

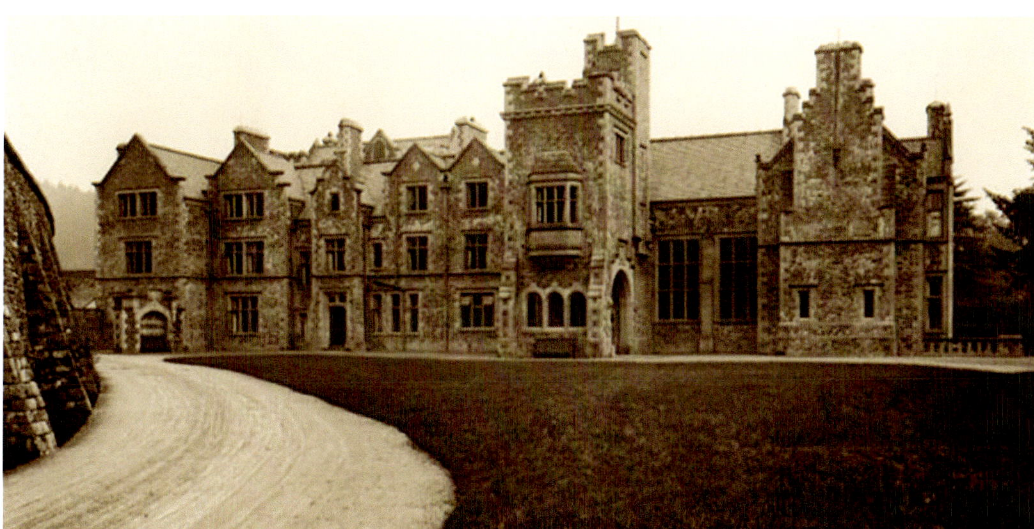

The entrance front of Grizedale Hall.

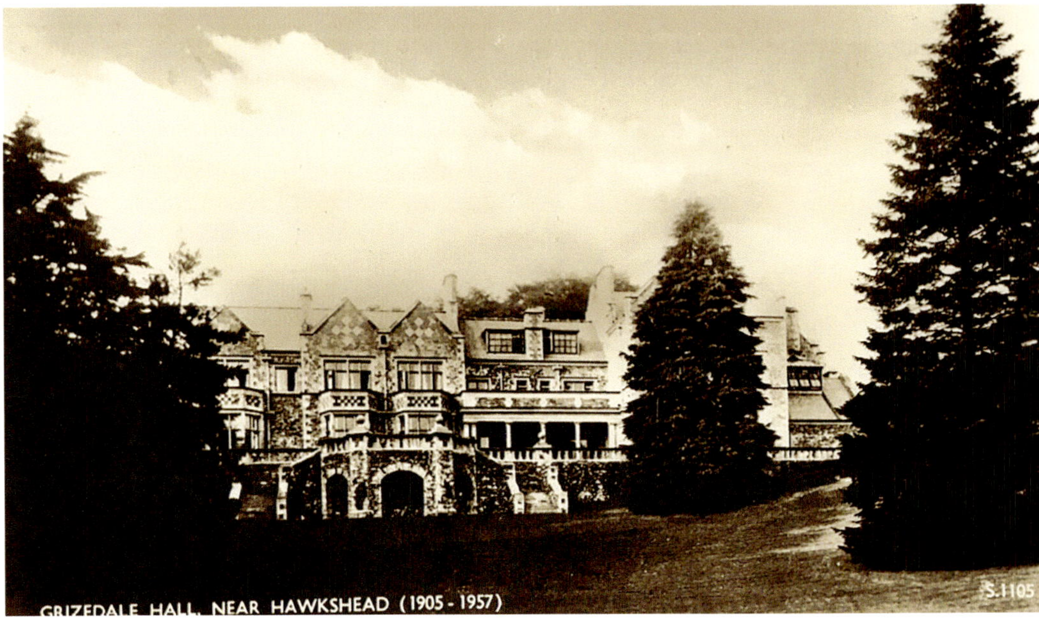


Grizedale Hall.

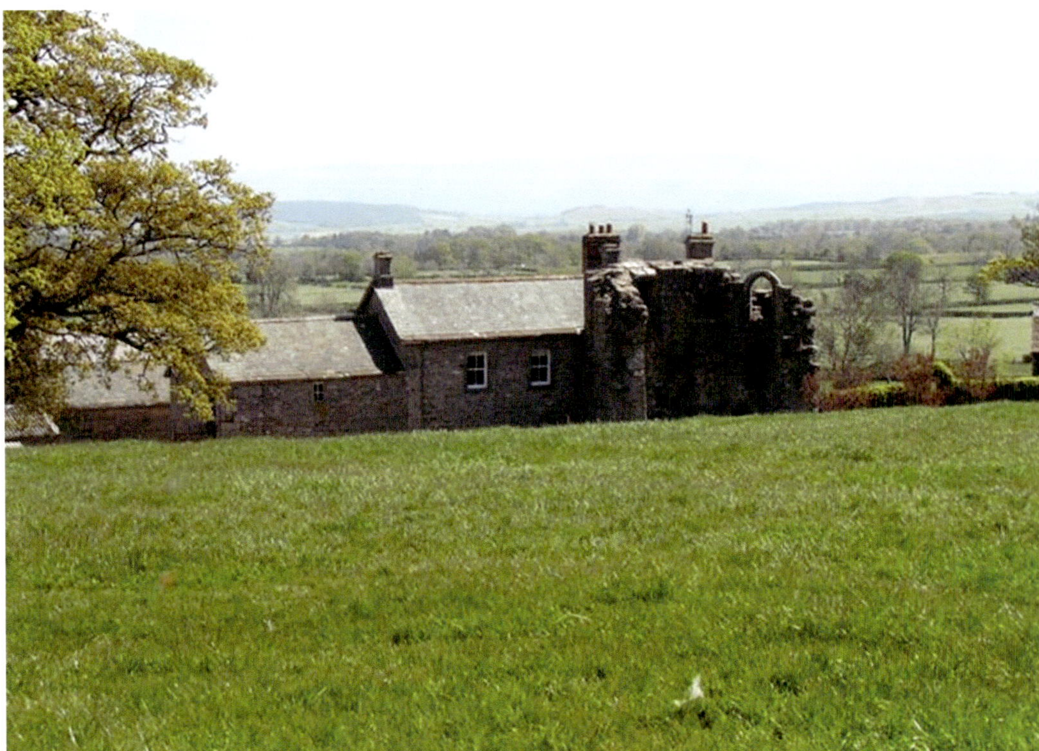

Hardrigg Hall.

## Hardrigg Hall, Skelton

The Boyvill family held the manor of Skelton in the twelfth century. What remains of Hardrigg Hall are parts of a fourteenth century or later solar tower, which was once the seat of the Southaike (Southiac) family, locally prominent from the thirteenth century and who acquired part of the Boyvill manor in 1272 when it was divided between co-heiresses. Hardrigg was sold to the Fletcher family in the seventeenth century and descended from them to the Vanes. Only fragments remain attached to a nineteenth-century farmhouse.

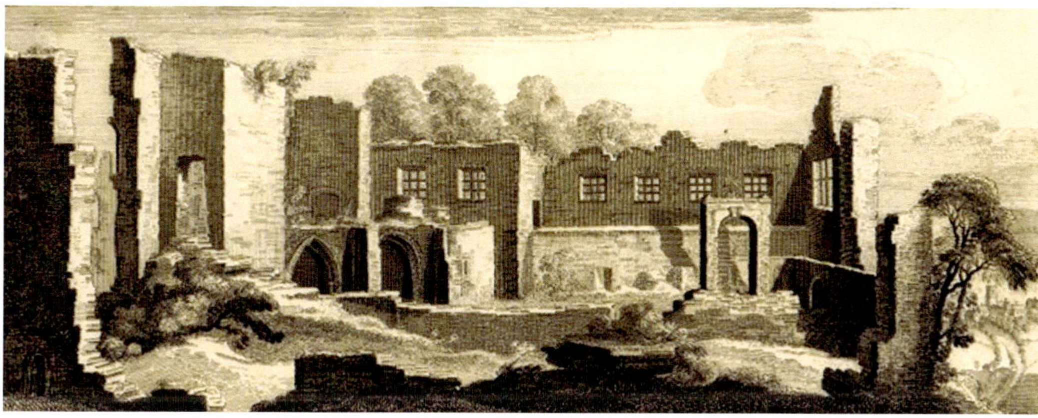

Hartley Castle.

## Hartley Castle, Kirkby Stephen

There is little now to suggest that Hartley Castle was once a grand Elizabethan mansion. In 1315 Hartley was confiscated from Roger de Clifford and granted to Andrew de Harcla (in English, Harclay or Hartley). De Harcla fortified the manor house in the early fourteenth century, but was hanged, drawn and quartered on the orders of Edward II in 1323 for collusion with the Scots. The manor passed to Ralph Neville of Raby and was sold by him to Thomas Musgrave, who was granted a licence to crenellate in 1353. Hartley Castle was extended during the early sixteenth century by Richard de Musgrave when two wings were added, and enlarged further by the Royalist Sir Phillip Musgrave after the restoration. When Thomas Machel visited the castle in 1677 it consisted of an inner courtyard surrounded by three- or four-storey buildings, with an outer court containing service rooms and protected by a curtain wall. There was a chapel, long gallery with oriel window and a range of state apartments. Despite this splendour, the castle was abandoned in the late seventeenth century when the Musgraves moved to Eden Hall and demolished in the first half of the eighteenth. All that remains are earthworks, a few metres of wall and the stairs down to a vaulted cellar for the former kitchen. A late eighteenth-century farmhouse stands on the site.

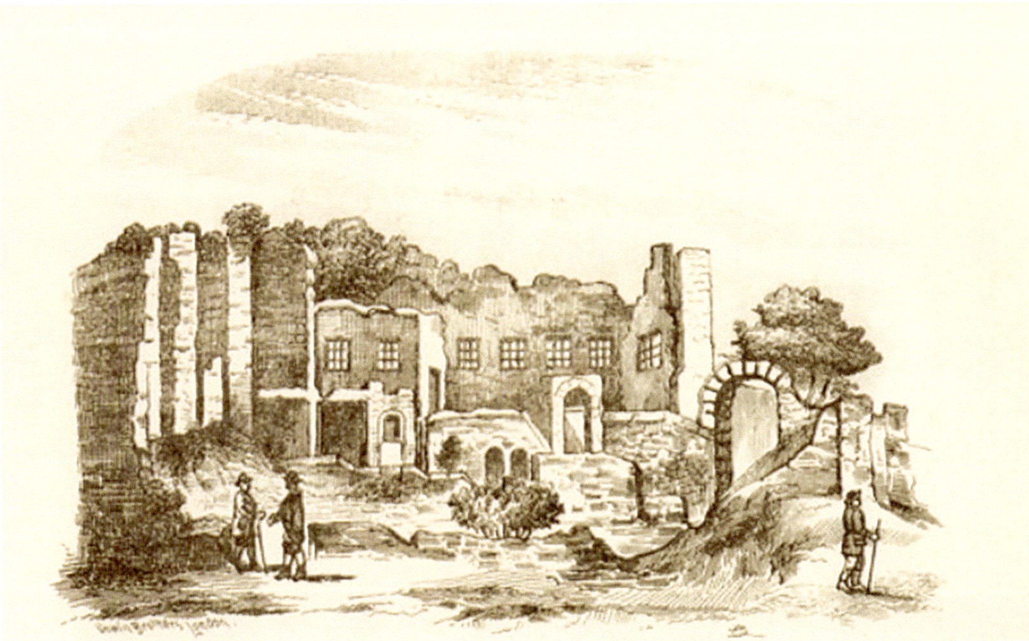

Hartley Castle.

## Helsfell Hall, Kendal

Helsfell was an early sixteenth-century house, probably built for Robert Briggs, a clothier and landlord from a long-established local family. In *The Annals of Kendal* by Cornelius Nicholson (1871) Helsfell is described as 'once a place of considerable importance'. The hall passed to the Philipsons of Hollin Hall, who owned it until the early eighteenth century. The Pigeons and the Days followed before it passed to the Burninghams in 1804. From 1874 Helsfell was part of the Underley estate and a new farmhouse was built nearby. The hall was often tenanted and an attached cottage was built whilst the hall itself fell into dereliction. What survives is probably a former cross wing of the original hall, which is now used as a barn. The remains of the hall have been conserved and later additions demolished. In the middle of the nineteenth century a collection of ancient bones, including those of a wolf, were found in a nearby cave.

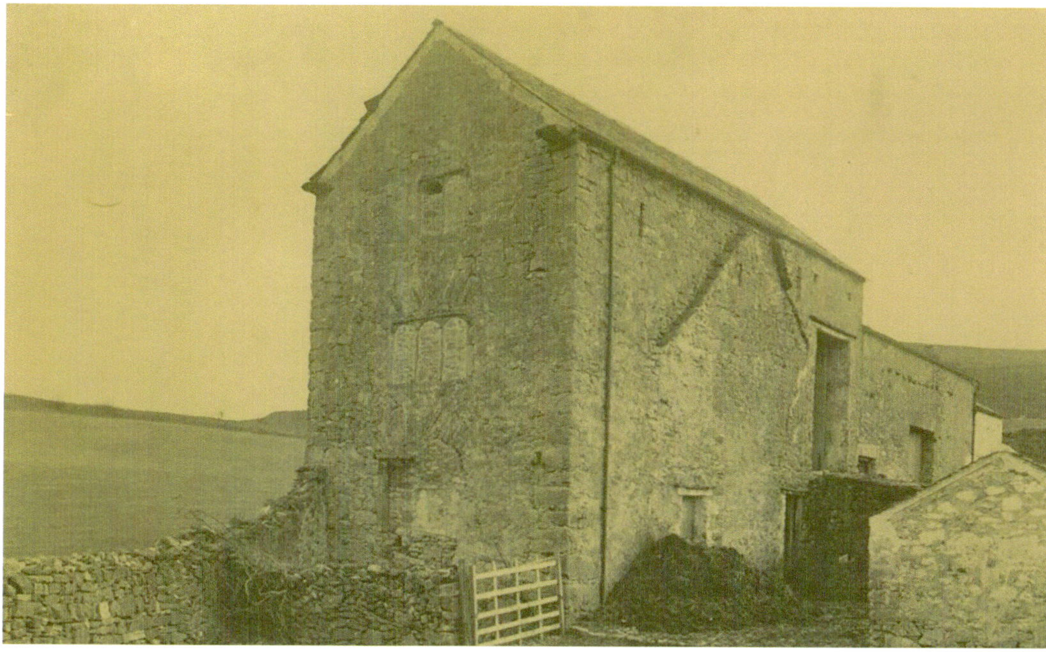

Helsfell Hall.

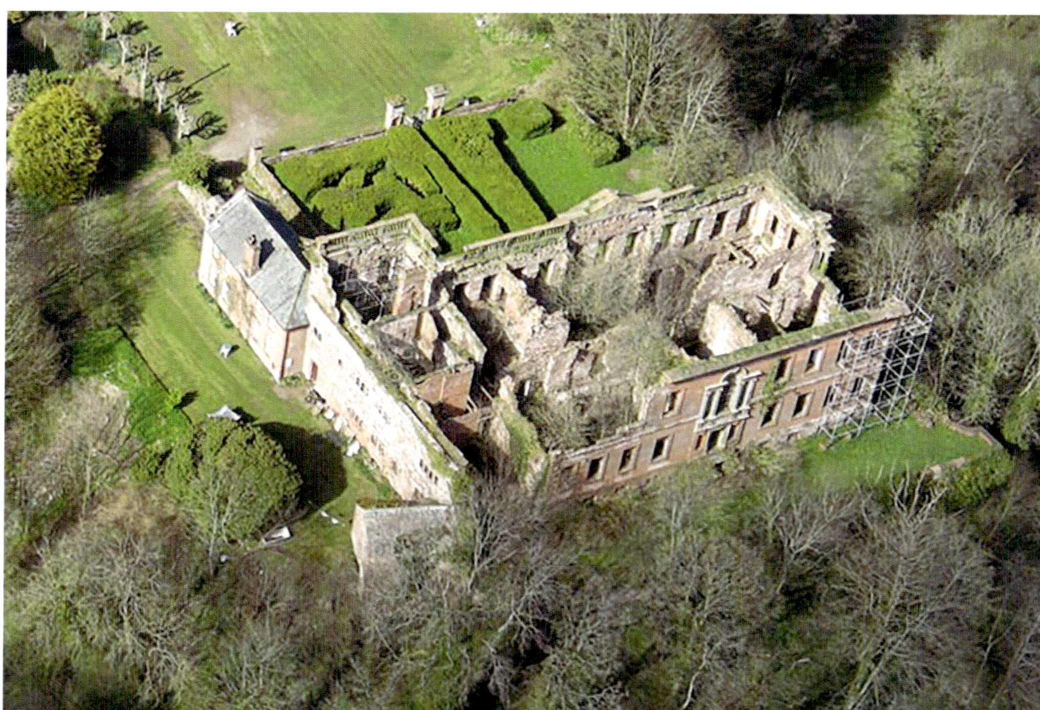

Aerial view of High Head Castle.

## High Head Castle, Ivegill

High Head Castle (also known as High Head Castle) was gutted by fire in 1956 and has hovered on the brink of restoration ever since. The house began as a fortified manor house and is recorded as early as 1272. In 1313 it was granted to John de Harcla. Like so many Cumbrian houses, the core was a pele tower surrounded by a curtain wall. Sir William L'Engleys, Chief Forester of Inglewood from 1328, acquired High Head and was succeeded by his son Sir William, whose daughter and heir, Isabel, married Nicholas Harrington. The Richmond family bought High Head from the Restwold family in the late sixteenth century and added a new wing to the medieval building. The older part of their house remains, with characteristic mullioned windows with round-arched lights under hood moulds. Attached to the south-west corner of this wing is the basement of the pele tower.

In the early eighteenth century Highhead was owned by Isabella, widow of Christopher Richmond, whose only son to grow to adulthood died at the age of twenty-six. Her grandson Henry Richmond Brougham became her designated successor at High Head and the family's other estates, but half the property was to be enjoyed by her unmarried daughter, Susanna, for her life, and the other half Susanna was to have until Henry Richmond Brougham came of age; in the event of Brougham dying before he came of age, the whole property would pass to the descendants of Isabella's daughter Susannah. Between 1744 and 1748 Richmond

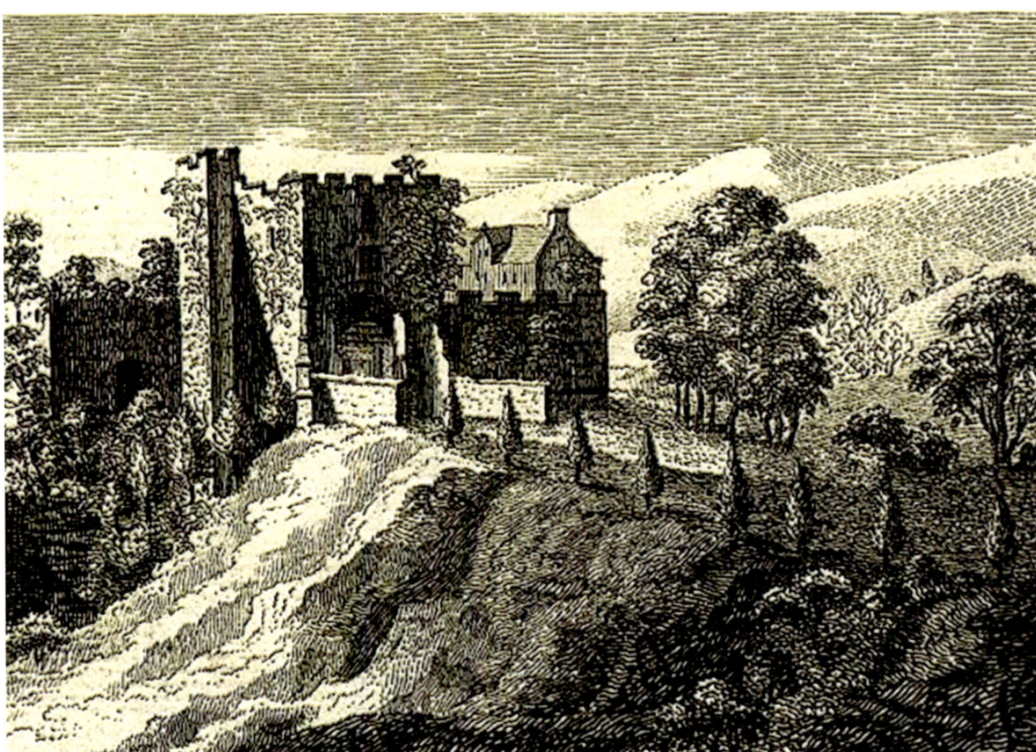

High Head Castle. (Samuel and Nathaniel Buck)

Brougham demolished two fourteenth-century towers and, under the guidance of his uncle, John Brougham, built a dramatic new wing, eleven bays long, with a three-bay centre under a pediment and a walled front court with an arch with paired Ionic columns. It has been suggested, for want of any plausible alternative, that the architect of the new house was James Gibbs. A local architect under the influence of Gibbs seems more likely. Work on the new house was brought to an abrupt end by the early death of Richmond Brougham, whereupon the property passed under the terms of the will to Susannah's daughters. Quarrelling amongst themselves over its ownership, none chose to live there. The house was in use as a farm and demolition had begun when, in 1820, Lord Chancellor Brougham bought first half and then the remainder of the property. Despite this promising new start, by 1860 interior panelling had been removed to Brougham Hall and the house was let as a farmhouse.

The second Lord Brougham carried out repairs to High Head between 1868 and 1874, but his son sold it in 1902 to Herbert Augustus Hills, a distinguished judge, for £18,000. Hills restored High Head, completing the north wing and proudly putting his initials over the main entrance. His architect was J. H. Martindale of Penrith. Hill was succeeded by his son Major John Hills MP, who sold High Head to fund the career of his son Andrew, first and last baronet, who died in 1955. The purchaser in 1935 was Alan Dower MP, who made High Head his home until 1950, when he lost his seat in Parliament and the hall was put up for sale but found no buyer. For much of this time High Head was tenanted. When the house burned down in 1956, it was the property of Mr Gordon Robinson, a Penrith butcher. In the 1960s, William Dickman, who was refused permission to demolish, lived in the surviving servants' wing built by Judge Hills. Christopher

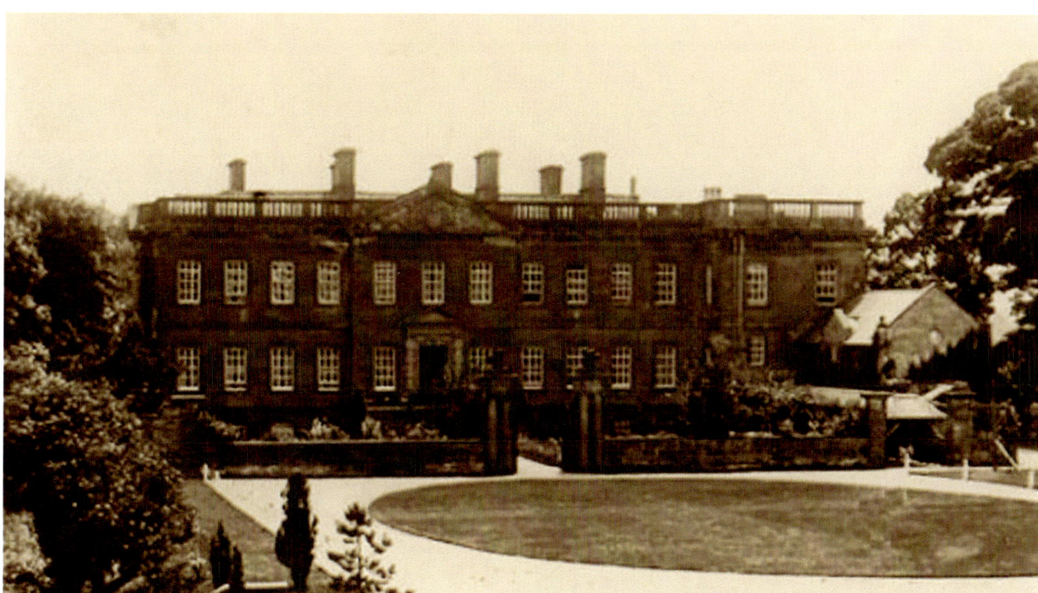

High Head Castle.

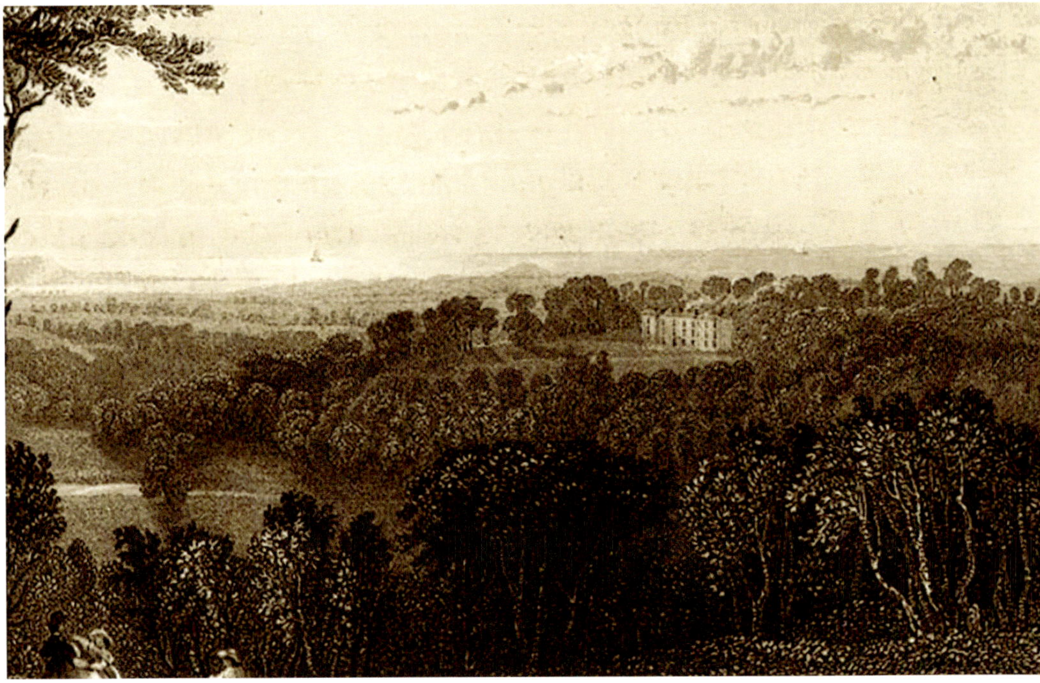

Holmrook Hall.

Terry, saviour of Brougham, bought High Head in 1987. Since then, considerable attempts have been made, by Terry and later owners, to restore High Head to its former glory.

Although the architect is unknown, surviving photographs indicate an interior of considerable quality. There was a vaulted corridor on the ground floor, with rooms on either side and colonnades opening onto the entrance hall and stairs. The drawing room had superb woodwork and panelling under a rococo ceiling with three shepherd putti.

A fine stable quadrangle with heavy rustication and cupola stands near the ruins of the house, which looms high over the River Petteril: the defensive capability of the original site is apparent. The rear façade has a superb Venetian window with Corinthian columns.

## Holmrook (Holme) Hall, Drigg

Holmrook Hall was once owned by Revd Charles Skeffington Lutwidge, whose relative Charles Lutwidge Dodgson – better known as Lewis Carroll – was a regular visitor. Charles Lutwidge, Comptroller General of the Coasts of Cumberland and Westmoreland, bought the property in 1759 and it remained in the family until the mid-twentieth century. Admiral Skeffington Lutwidge commanded HMS *Carcass* on its polar expedition during which midshipman Horatio Nelson singlehandedly took on a polar bear in an attempt to obtain its pelt for his father. In its final form, the house dated from the middle of the eighteenth century, with nine bays and three storeys, two bays at each end projecting slightly forwards with tripartite

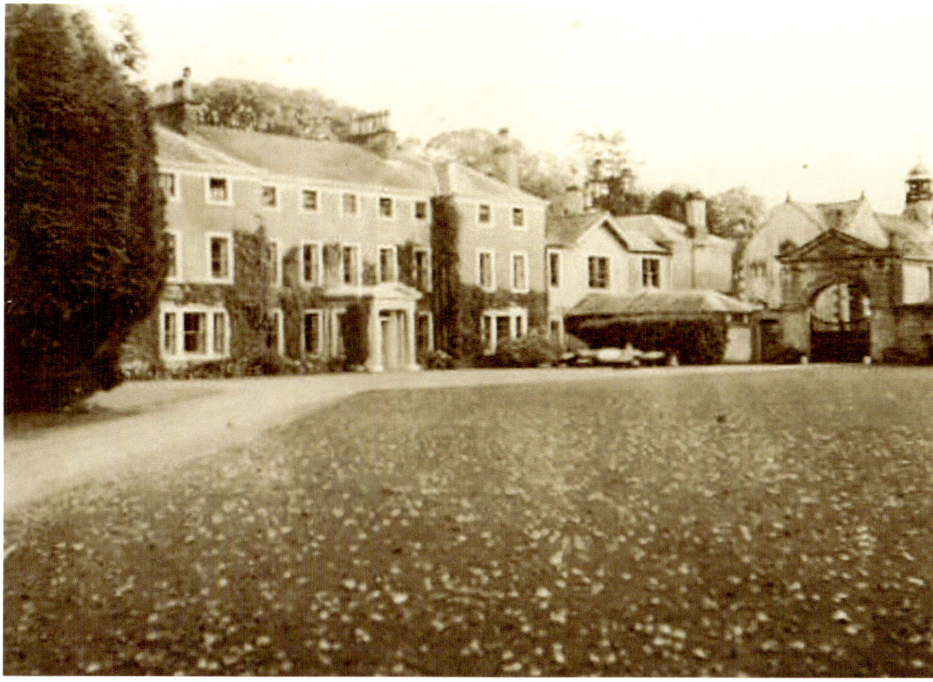

Holmrook Hall.

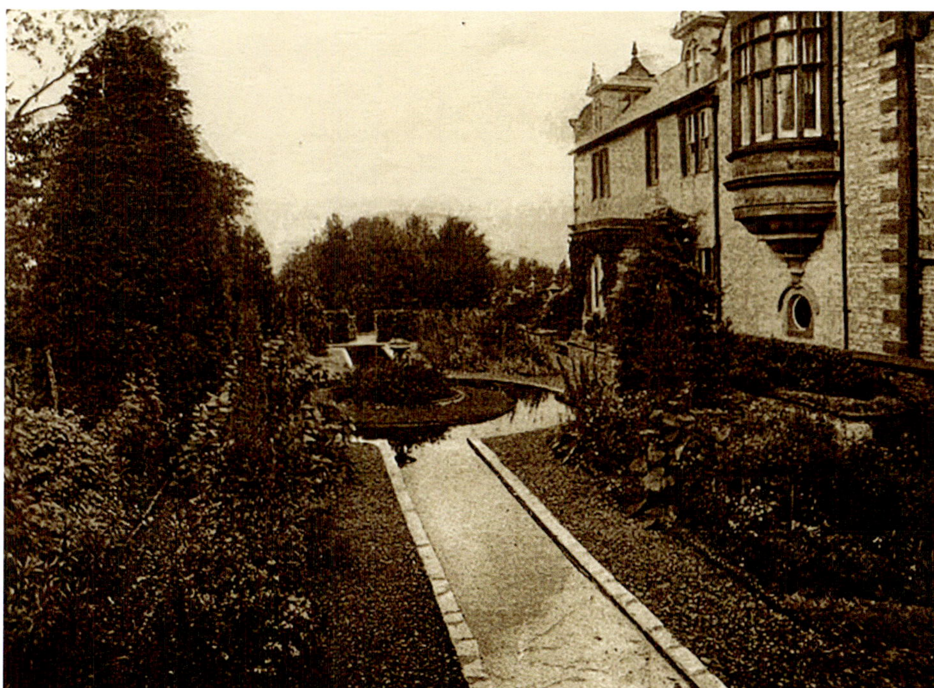

Hwith.

windows on the ground floor. Alterations were carried out by Mervyn Macartney in the early twentieth century.

During the Second World War Holmrook Hall was used by the Royal Navy. Locals were told that it was a rest home for shipwrecked and distressed sailors but in truth it was the Royal Navy bomb and munitions training school between 1943 and 1946, and known as HMS Volcano. Amongst its pupils were members of the US Navy and Norwegian Resistance. The hall was chosen because of its remote location, as well as its proximity to the munitions works at Drigg. The courageous individuals tasked with clearing mines that might hamper the D-Day landings also trained at Holmrook. The hall fell into disrepair after the war and was demolished in 1956. The stables survive and have been converted into housing.

## Hwith, Ravenstonedale

Hwith was built between 1869 and 1875 by Joseph Bintley for John Hewetson. The house's unusual name is an acronym of the names of John and his brothers in order of age (Henry, William, John Thomas and Humphrey – John supplied the 'I' (commonly interchangeable with a 'j' in inscriptions) and 't'. Born in a farmhouse near Ravenstonedale in 1806, John was apprenticed to a London draper but aged twenty-two established his own upholstery business on Tottenham Court Road in partnership with his brothers. Becoming wealthy, the Hewetsons had a London home overlooking Regent's Park and John was in a position to build himself

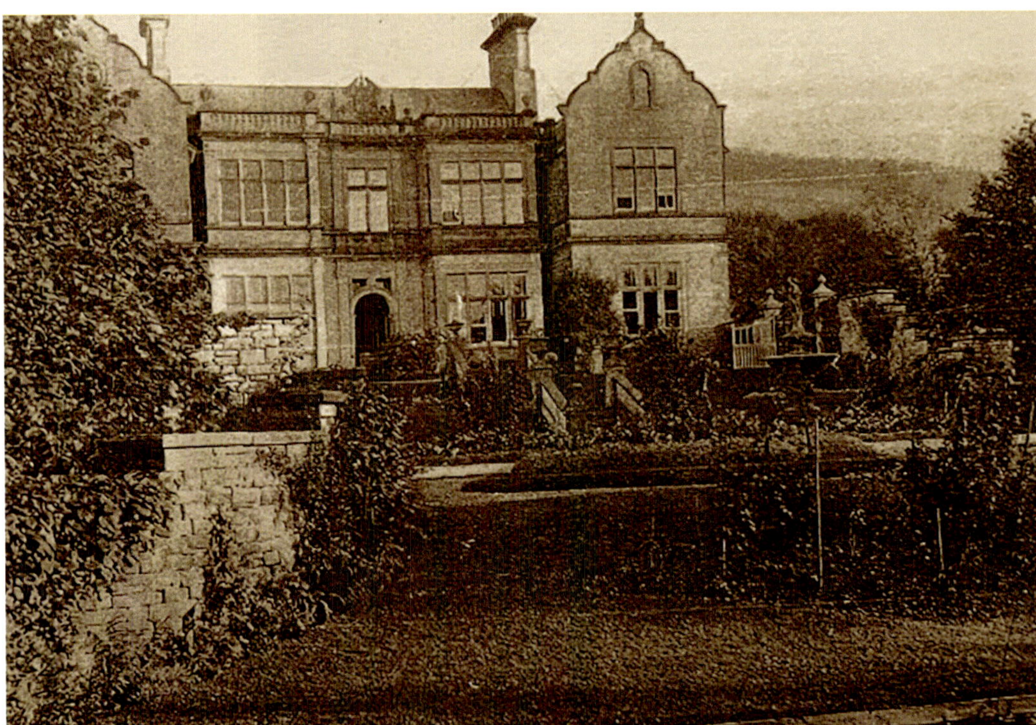

Hwith.

a retirement home near the village of his birth. Sadly, he died in 1876, having enjoyed his new home for only a year. His son Harold and widow Adelaide were living at Hwith in 1911 and on her death in 1923 the property was put up for sale. No buyer could be found and the house was demolished in 1927.

Hwith was Jacobean in style and symmetrical, looking not unlike a pair of grand suburban semidetached houses. Fragments of the formal gardens remain. Plans were prepared by Quinlan Terry for a new house, but planning permission has not been granted.

## Ireby Grange, High Ireby

Ireby Grange was originally the seat of the Grainger family. Jane Grainger left the house and estate to her cousin Henry Grainger, a merchant with interests in Liverpool. In 1847 Henry Grainger and his son John used the house only as an occasional residence, but in 1866 and in need of cash, Henry put the property on the market. In 1870 the Grange was bought by John Boustead, an Army agent. In the 1880s Boustead let the estate for shooting before it was sold in 1906 to the Gurneys, who still own it and are noted local benefactors through the Gurney Charitable Trust. Henry Grainger's son became agent-general for South Australia and had in turn one son who died without issue, the male line of the Graingers coming to an end on his death.

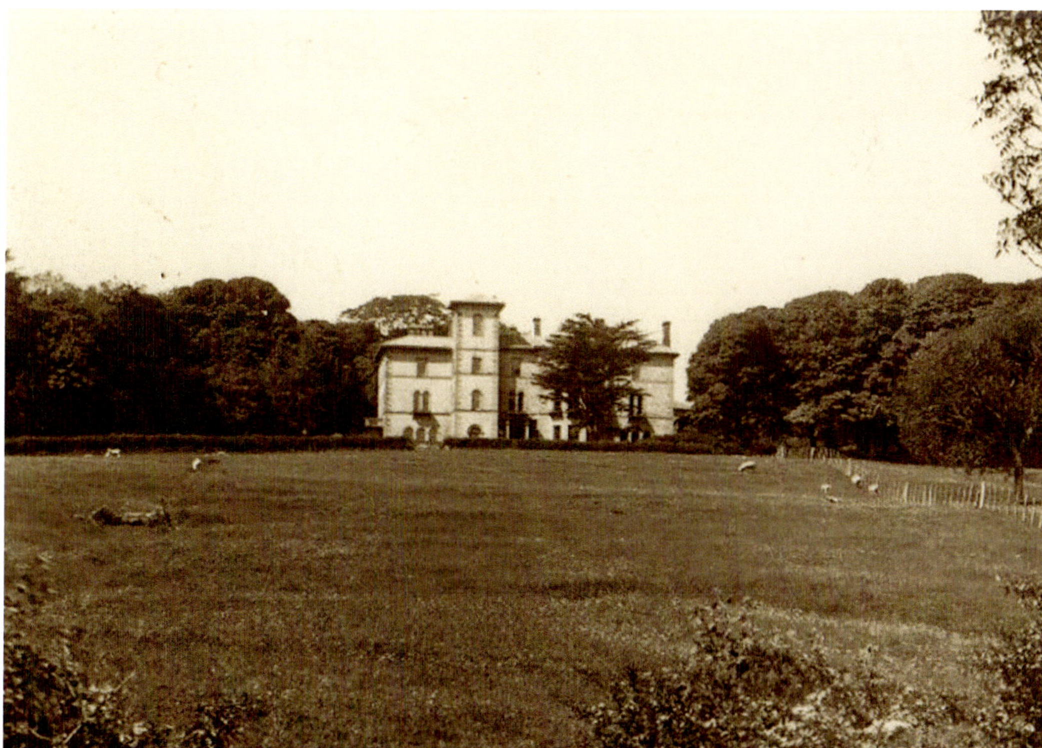

Ireby Grange.

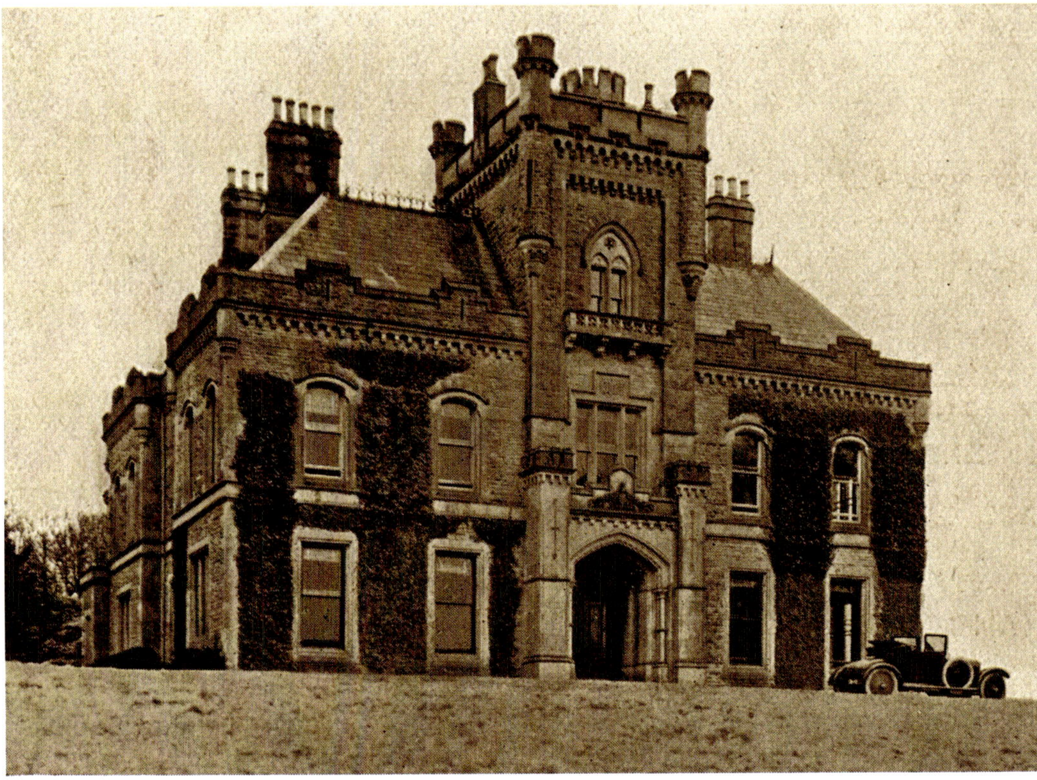

Killhow.

The house was built in an Italianate style with a prominent campanile-style tower. The ground floor contained a large paved hall, a dining room (later used as a library) and a morning room, which later became the dining room. The service wings were at this level whilst, due to a fall in the surrounding land, the first floor contained the drawing and billiard rooms, which had direct access to the gardens, as well as the principal bedrooms. On the top floor were a further ten bedrooms and dressing rooms. The house was surrounded by extensive formal gardens with terraces, a lake, a shrubbery and a woodland walk.

When the novelist Hugh Walpole, who lived on the shores of Derwentwater, visited Ireby in 1931, he found the house in poor condition and used it as the model for the main house in *The Fortress*, the third in his once phenomenally popular Rogue Herries series of novels. Ireby was destroyed by fire on 18 January 1957. At that time, the house belonged to Norman Gurney, a retired land agent from London who used it for summer holidays, occupying only a handful of its fifty-two rooms. Norman had inherited the property from his father James. Stone from the ruins was later used to fill in nearby disused mineshafts. The ancillary buildings have been converted into holiday properties.

## Killhow, Ireby

Killhow was demolished in 1926. The house had been built in a vaguely Gothic style by John Porter Foster, a London draper of Cumbrian birth who retired to his home county, at a cost of £36,000, in 1865. By 1871, the widowed Foster was living at Killhow with his unmarried daughter Hannah and on his death in 1878 the property passed to his son Samuel, who was a barrister and repeatedly unsuccessful Conservative parliamentary candidate. In 1913 plans were considered for turning the empty house into a sanatorium for sufferers from tuberculosis, but the scheme was not approved and the house passed to John Foster, Samuel's son and the last of the Fosters. John was unmarried and a barrister like his father with a practice in London and Cairo; he died in Luxor in 1920 when the house and estate of 1,592 acres were once again put on the market. Failing to sell, in 1926 the house was put up for sale 'at a ridiculously low figure to avoid demolition'. Even this was not enough to save it and Killhow was sold for £2,000 to Haigh Wilson of Ripon for demolition. The property was parcelled into lots including 15,000 local slates, 65,000 bricks, mantelpieces, parquet flooring and a stained-glass window. Only the gateposts of Killhow, which lasted barely fifty years as a grand residence, survive.

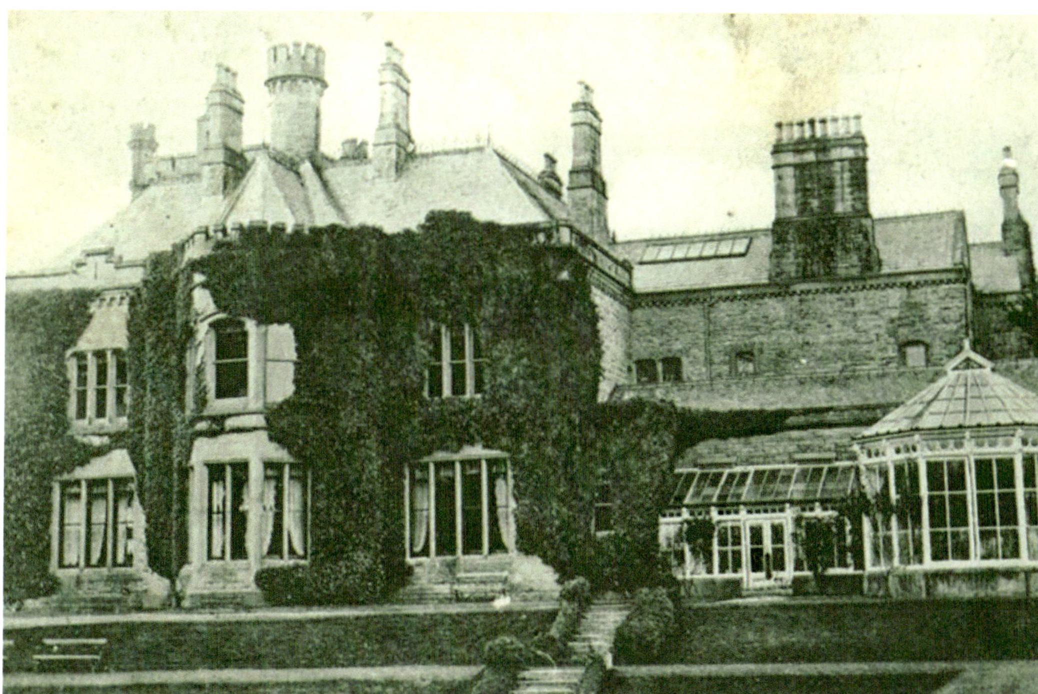

Killhow.

## Kingmoor House (Deer Park House), Carlisle

The original owner of the land on which Kingmoor House was built is said to have committed suicide when the railway was built across his land. W. E. Bell was the tenant of Kingmoor House until 1940, when the property was purchased by the Caledonian Railway, which used it as a hostel for its staff, which it remained until the mid-1950s, after which it was divided into flats. Kingmoor House was knocked down in the early 1970s.

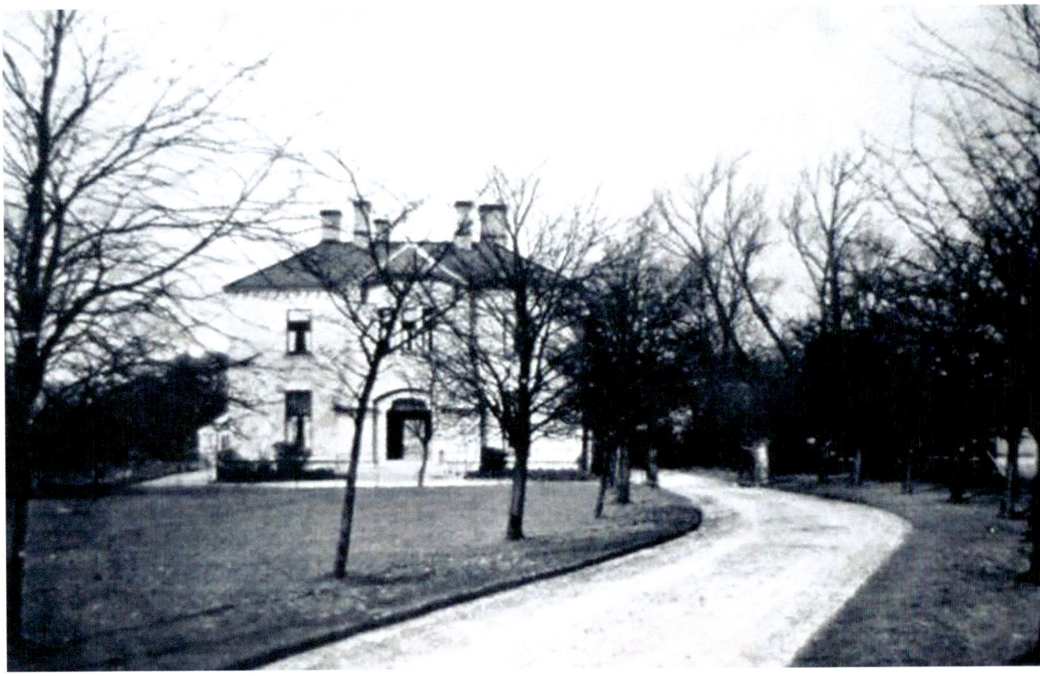

Kingmoor House.

## Kirklinton Hall, Kirklinton

Richard de Boyville built Levington Castle in the early twelfth century. The de Boyvilles owned the estate until 1272 and various families followed until Edmund Appleby bought Kirklinton from Sir Edward Musgrave in 1661, demolished the castle and built his late seventeenth-century five-bay house, which remains at the core of the additions made to either side in the eighteenth century. Kirklinton remained the seat of the Dacre-Applebys until 1868 when, on the death of Joseph Dacre, it was sold to the Saul family. Extensions were made in the Jacobethan style in 1875 to the designs of Cory and Ferguson, which doubled the size of the house. In its final form Kirklinton became a rather amorphous L shape.

The property was put on the market in 1939, but failing to find a buyer, the estate was broken up. The hall was an RAF base during the Second World War and in 1948 it was bought by Doris and Willie Hay, who used it as a nightclub and casino, which attracted many of the less salubrious members of gangster society. Kirklinton fell into ruin in the 1970s. Mr and Mrs Boyle bought the property in

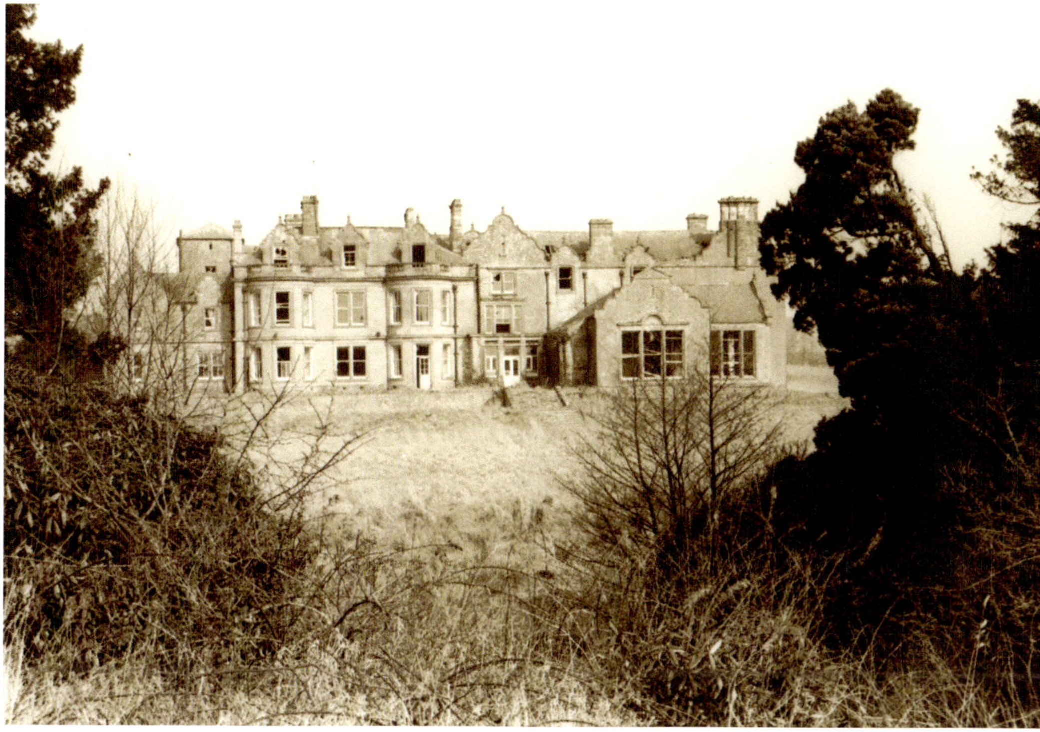

Kirklinton before restoration began.

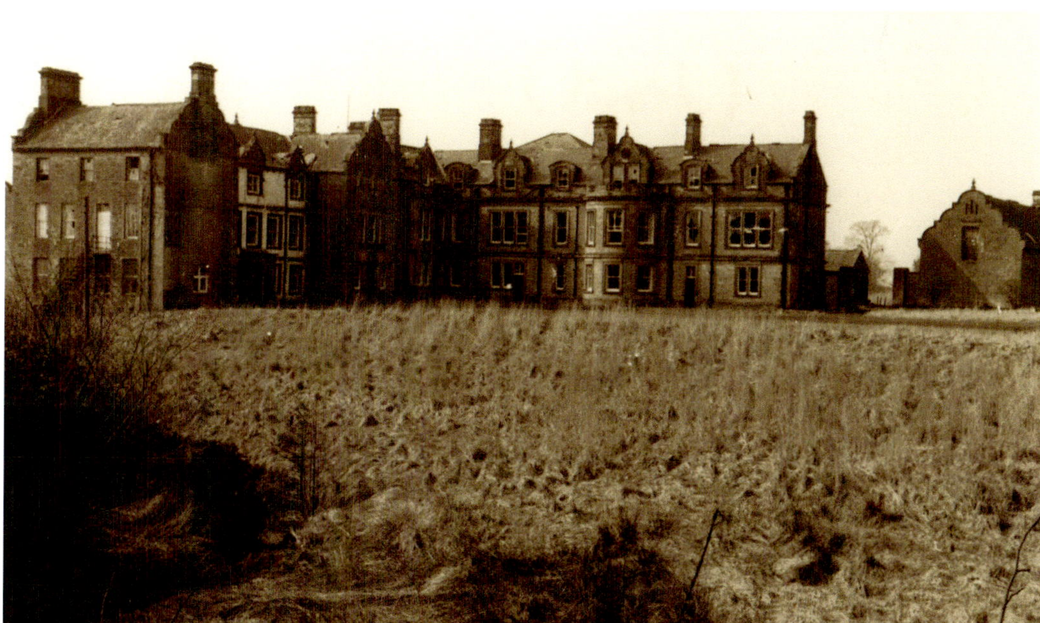

Kirklinton. The original house is on the left between two prominent Dutch gables.

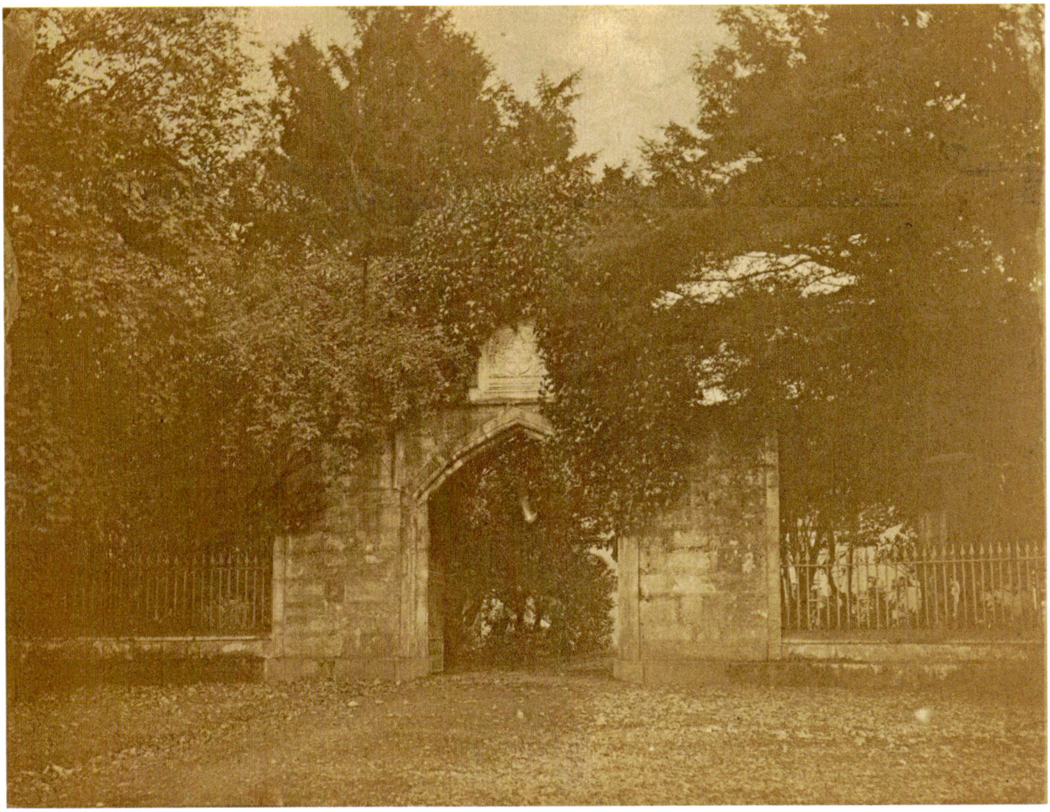

Lamplugh Hall gate.

2013 and have begun the process of restoration of the hall and gardens. Kirklinton is now a wedding and events venue and the house and gardens are open to the public.

## Lamplugh Hall, Lamplugh

Lamplugh was the seat of the Lamplugh family from the reign of Henry II. It (inevitably) included a pele tower extended by John Lamplugh in 1595. On the death of Thomas Lamplugh in 1737 the house passed to another Thomas Lamplugh, grandson of the archbishop of York, from whom it passed to the Roper and Brooksbank families. The tower was complete when it was drawn by George Monkhouse, whose drawing also shows the Elizabethan house. The building appears to have been demolished in 1821 when it was described as 'a bulky square building with high ramparts, and extremely massive, with walls nine feet thick.' The tower, which was replaced by a rather grand farmhouse, was apparently so strong that dynamite was used to demolish it. The surviving gatehouse was mostly rebuilt in 1961 after a yew tree fell on it, although the earlier datestone (1595) was retained. The present house stands on the site of the Elizabethan hall and may include elements of it and earlier buildings.

## Lowther Hall, Penrith

The Lowthers have been settled in the top right corner of Cumbria since at least the twelfth century. Like all the great northern families they played an active role in skirmishes on either side of the border with Scotland and by marriage, purchase and canny business sense became and remain one of the great landed families of the north. The Lowthers descend from Dolfin, who settled at Lowther around 1150, although a claim has been made to a pre-Conquest descent. In 1283 Sir Hugh Lowther, lawyer and MP, was given permission to impark his estate. The first house on the site, of which no images survive, must have been a pele or defensive tower around which later buildings would be added and which replaced an earlier motte and bailey recently identified by archaeology in the park. As so common in Cumbria, this first house would follow the typical hall and defensive cross ranges plan. The Lowther estate grew throughout the early medieval period and family members played increasingly prominent roles in national affairs, defending the border, serving in parliament and fighting in the king's wars, including at Agincourt where Sir Hugh Lowther served alongside his monarch. This first Lowther Hall played host to Mary Queen of Scots in 1568 on her way to Bolton Castle from Carlisle Castle where Sir Richard Lowther was deputy captain.

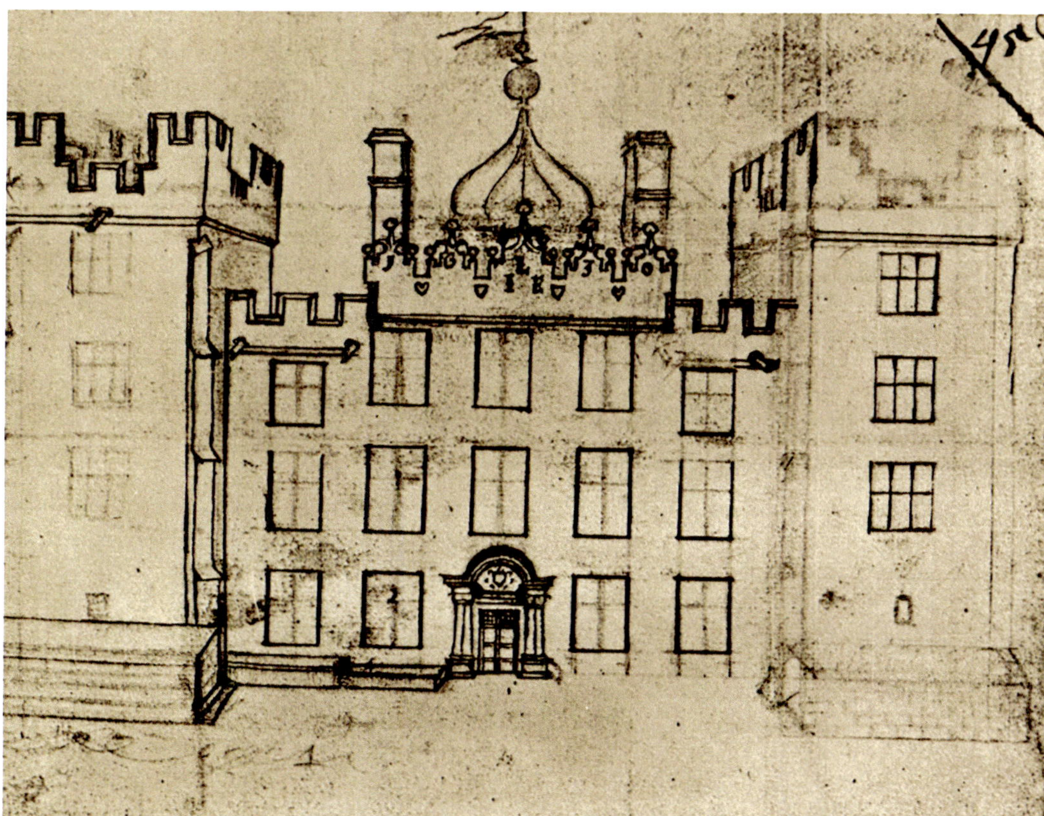

Lowther Hall drawn by Thomas Machell in 1630.

Between 1628 and 1630 Sir John Lowther rebuilt the central portion of his ancestral home in the form of a square block with corner turrets and a centrally placed dome, using timber from the great hall roof of Kirkoswald Castle. His son, also Sir John and first baronet, added a new west wing and porch around a decade later, and after a further decade added a matching wing containing a gallery. The wings and porch have been ascribed to William Pogmire. In 1691–92, the 1st Viscount Lonsdale demolished the centre of the house and built a thirteen-bay centre block between the mid-seventeenth-century wings. The architect for the new house was William Talman, although Lord Lonsdale would claim much of the credit.

Plans for the rebuilding were also sought from Colen Campbell and an unrealised design appears in *Vitruvius Britannicus*. James Gibbs was asked to prepare designs for modernising the house and rebuilding the wings in a more contemporary style. Unfortunately, the centre of the house was destroyed by fire in 1718 and despite further designs from Campbell and Gibbs, the Lowthers kept hold of their money and lived in the surviving wings.

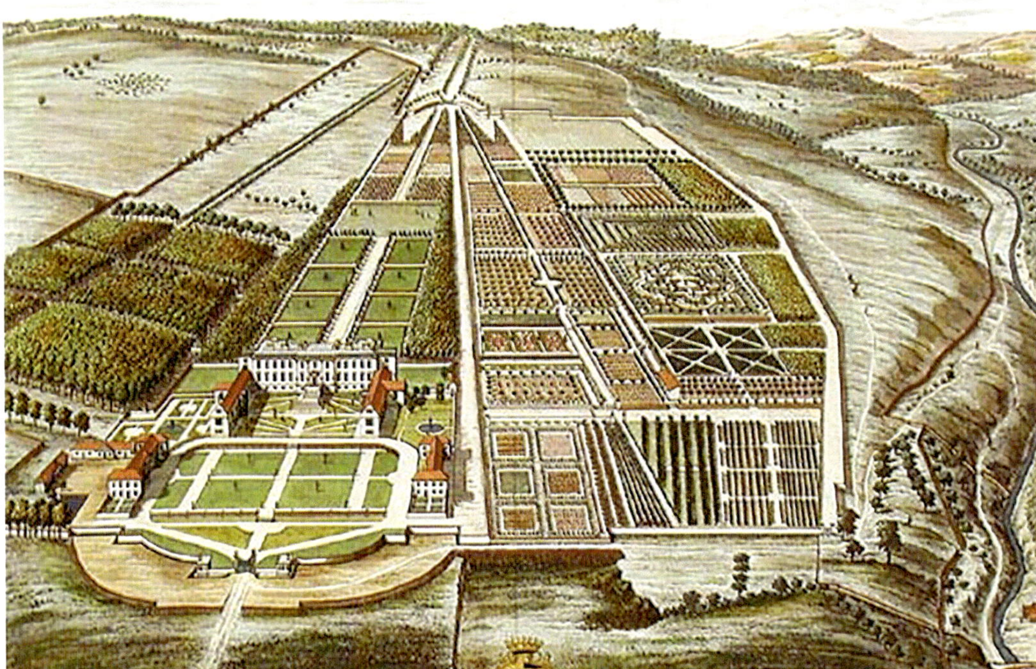

The 1st Viscount Lonsdale's House, illustrated by Kip in 1707. The new block and the earlier wings are clearly shown.

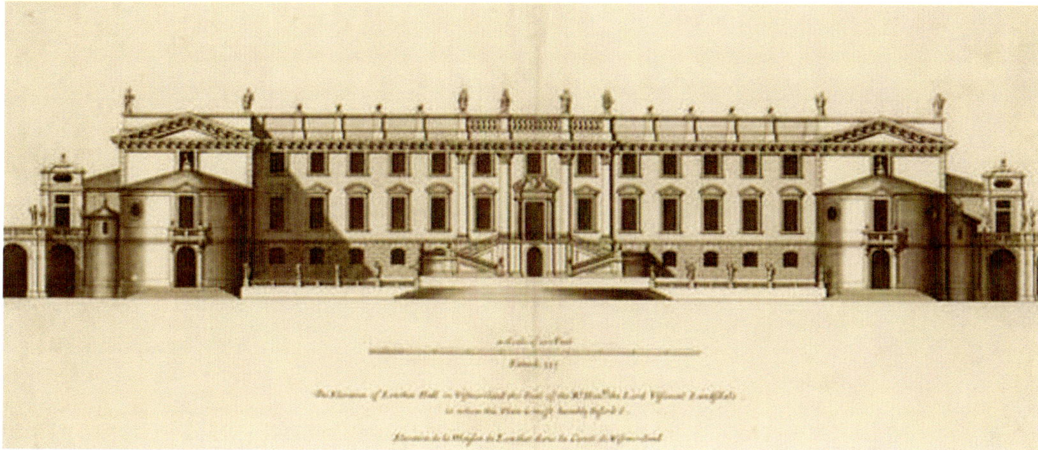

Colen Campbell's unbuilt design for Lowther Hall.

## Lowther Castle, Penrith

In 1731 the Lowther estates, ships, coal mines and political patronages passed to James, 1st Earl of Lonsdale, who shared the family propensity for adding unbuilt architectural designs from the leading architects of the day to a pile in the library; in his case from Matthew Brettingham (1759–1762), Capability Brown (1763), and a few years later both James and Robert Adam. Thomas Harrison produced designs around 1800 and, finally, around the same time, Francis Webster began the modernisation of the west wing. Webster's patron was Sir James Lonsdale, 'Wicked Jimmy' or 'Jemmy Grasp-all', 1st Earl of Lonsdale, a man of whom no one had anything good to say, who controlled absolutely nine seats in the House of Commons and kept the embalmed body of his mistress at his home at Maulds Meaburn for years after her early death. In life he became a local bogeyman and in death a phantom carriage drawn by Wicked Jimmy's ghost is said still to haunt Lowther Park. Jeremiah Sullivan says of Wicked Jimmy:

> [He] became a still greater terror to the country after death, than he had even been during his life. He was with difficulty buried; and whilst the clergyman was praying over him, he very nearly knocked the reverend gentleman from his desk. When placed in the grave, the power of creating alarm was not interred with his bones. There were disturbances in the Hall, noises in the stables; neither men nor animals were suffered to rest.

A collective local sigh of relief doubtless occurred when Sir William Lowther inherited in 1802 and in 1807 became 1st Earl of Lonsdale of the second (current) creation. Sir William would finally build a castle reflecting the local standing of the Lowthers. He was by all accounts a thoroughly decent man and a stark contrast to his predecessor: upon inheriting the estate he paid off the latter's debts to his employees and local workmen, including £4,000 of unpaid wages (with interest) to William Wordsworth's father, Sir James' political agent. Wordsworth would later dedicate his "Excursion" to the earl.

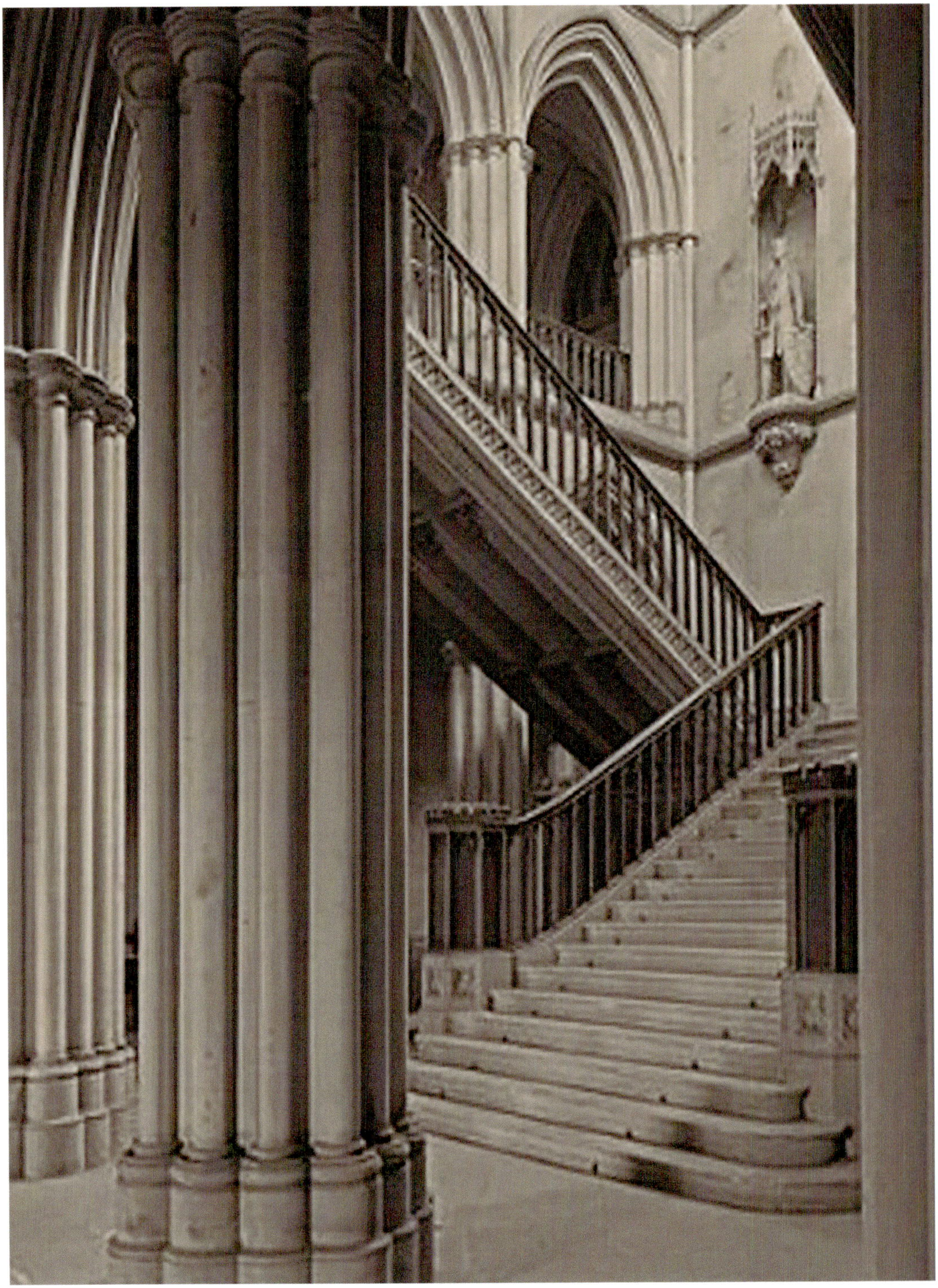

The stair hall of Lowther Castle

The new Earl of Lonsdale was a man of immense wealth and, despite his fundamental decency, was well aware of his local status. After casting around for a suitable architect, and on the recommendation of Charles Dance, who thought distant Cumberland too remote, he commissioned Robert Smirke to design the castle, the ruins of which still dominate the parkland at Lowther. It appears likely that Smirke's design bore a close resemblance to plans produced by Dance. Smirke would later go on to design the British Museum but Lowther was his first major commission.

Smirke began by remodelling the surviving service rooms and building a new stable court in 1806. In 1809 the Lowthers moved into the east wing and the central block was finished in 1811. The west wing was complete by 1813, although minor work continued for another decade. By 1814, building Lowther Castle had cost £77,000 (£4.5 million at today's values) in materials and labour. However, much of the raw materials had been taken from the estate; Smirke estimated that had this not been the case the total cost would have come to £150,000. Sculpture galleries, one of which survives and has been restored, were added by James Mawson in 1866.

In the castle's early days, artists and poets were warmly welcomed by Lowther and his wife Augusta. Wordsworth, who became a friend, described

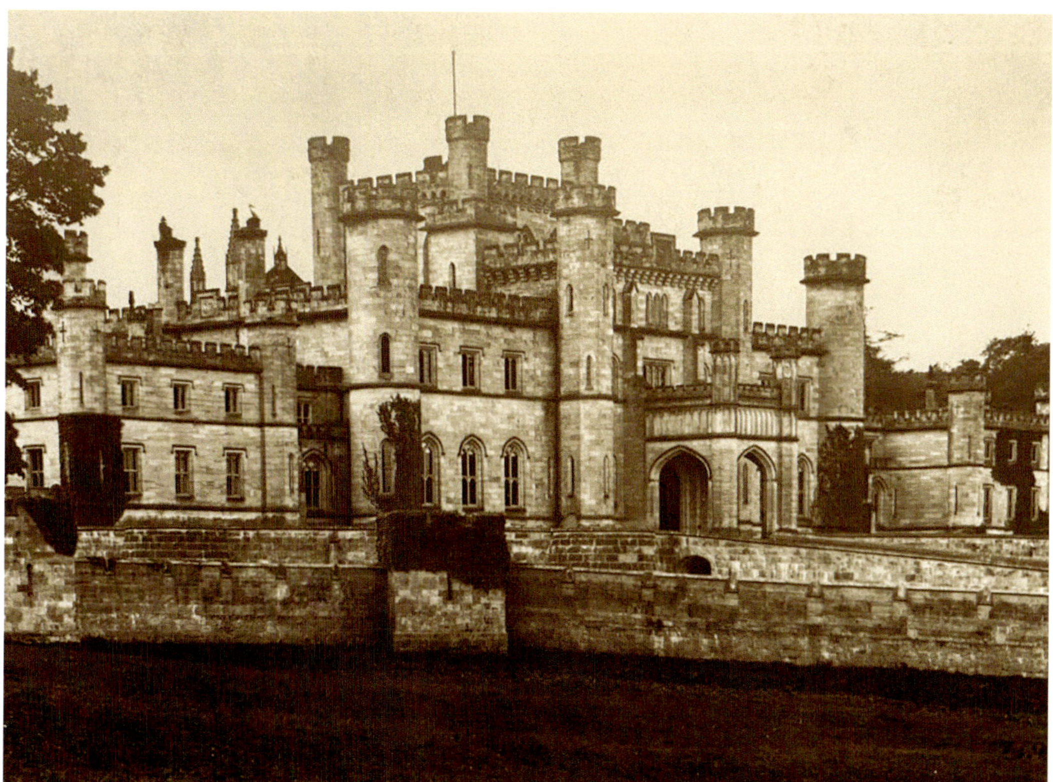

Lowther Castle's entrance front.

the house in a not very good poem as a 'majestic pile' of 'cathedral pomp and grace'. J. M. W. Turner was also encouraged to stay. His painting of the castle in 1810, when it was still under construction, hangs in the Bowes Museum. The nineteenth-century Lowthers had the money and taste to collect paintings and a list of artworks adorning the walls of Lowther compiled in 1850 includes works by Breughel, Holbein, Rembrandt, Rubens, Titian, and Vandyke.

The house was designed with the notion of hospitality squarely in mind: it was said (incorrectly) that there was a room for every day of the year. For just over a century, entertainment in abundance was the premier function of Lowther Castle and the Lowthers lived in Ruritanian splendour. The castle could seat up to sixty or seventy guests at dinner; over the course of the nineteenth century, it saw a great many famous and influential figures pass through its halls. It also played host to several European leaders, among them Kaiser Wilhelm II and the kings of Italy and Portugal. British royalty were regular visitors and amongst less exalted guests was the royal mistress (and the earl's) Lillie Langtry.

Such grandeur was not to last. The accession of Hugh Lowther in 1882 as 5th Earl of Lonsdale proved disastrous to the family's finances and the future

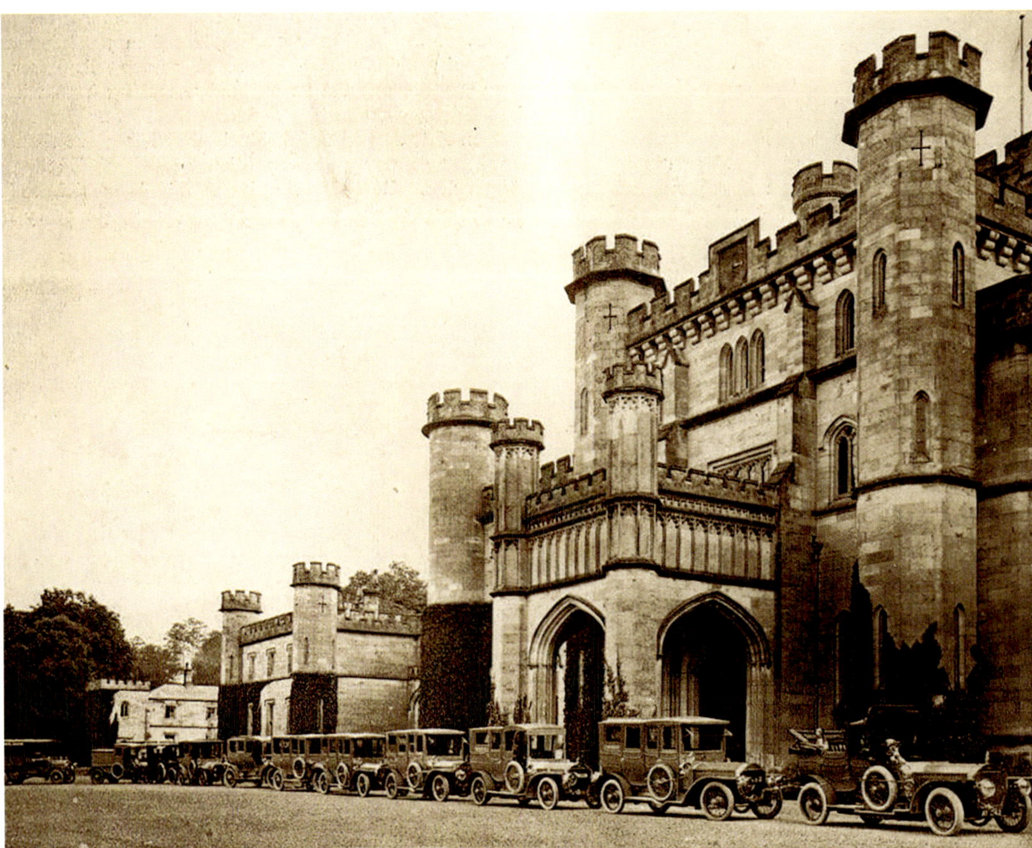

Lowther Castle with the Yellow Earl's fleet of cars.

prosperity of the castle. Hugh, younger son of the third earl, was never meant to inherit the estate, but the early death of his brother made him the heir to vast coal wealth, enormous estates, four great houses and an income approaching £4,000 a week! For the next fifty years he would extract every penny from this estate for his own personal pleasure. Indeed, the estate only survived because he had sold his revisionary interests to the trustees, with the result that they, to a degree, controlled him and not the other way round. As the 'Yellow Earl' or 'Lordy' his exploits and affairs, including a period as a rancher in Wyoming and touring with his own theatre company, made him legendary. Undoubtedly brave, he fought the world boxing champion Joe Sullivan and was a fearless horseman. Lordy's lovers included Lilly Langtry, he learned boxing from the champion of England Jem Mace, spent time with a travelling circus, hunted buffalo in America, travelled in Alaska and was honorary president of Arsenal Football Club. A fellow peer said of him that he was 'almost an emperor, but not quite a gentleman'. All his activities had one thing in common: they cost astonishing amounts of money. His cigar bill was £5,000 per annum and his dogs travelled in their own first-class railway carriage. He became a hugely popular public figure, a popularity that the more serious of his contemporaries (and his trustees) must have found difficult to stomach. He was, for all his undoubted charm and 'common touch', a liar (or at any rate someone economical with the truth when it suited him), a spendthrift and sufficiently indifferent to the plight of those whose dangerous labours funded his extravagant lifestyle to do little to improve their lot. Nevertheless, his *joie-de-vivre*, courtesy, generosity and essential kindness to individuals made him much loved. He blew his inheritance on, among other things, horses, carriages, cars and armies of servants. His name is remembered for the Lonsdale Belt, the Waterloo Cup, which he founded, and as an early member of the Automobile Association, which took the Lonsdale yellow as its colour. During the First World War Hugh Lowther raised his own battalion of the Border Regiment, which, naturally, he

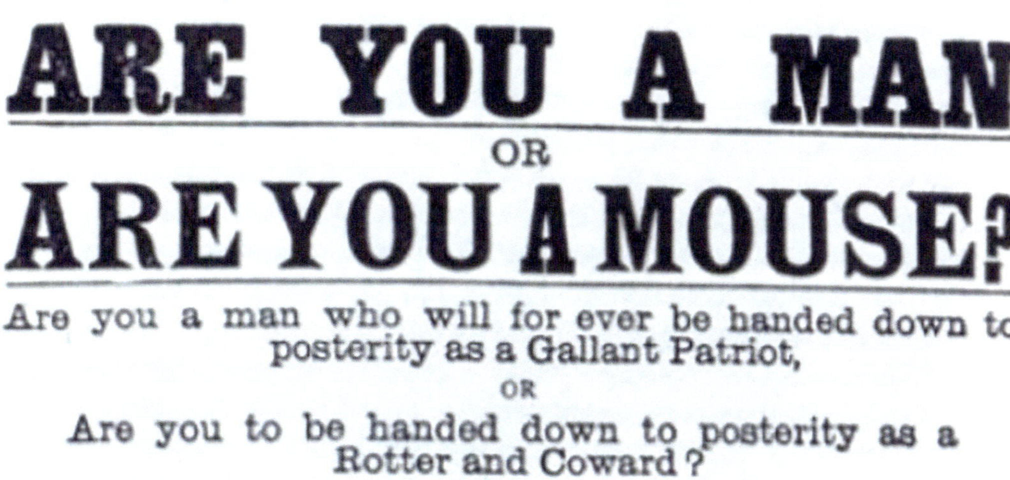


Lord Lonsdale's recruiting poster.

equipped with a different coloured uniform to other regiments. Lonsdale designed the regiment's recruiting poster, which was printed in yellow and began 'Are you a man or are you a mouse?'

Post-war financial pressures forced Lowther's sale of significant parts of his estates, and in 1926 the west Cumberland coal mines, which had provided much of the Lowther income, closed. The fifth earl closed the doors to his family's seat in 1935. During the Second World War the castle was requisitioned by the War Office as the base for an operation developing secret anti-tank weapons: the Canal Light Defence (CDL). King George VI, Earl Mountbatten, Eisenhower, and Churchill all visited Lowther Castle.

The Yellow Earl died childless in 1944, leaving his brother Lancelot, the sixth earl, a mountain of debt. In 1947, in the largest country house sale of the twentieth century, lasting twenty-two days, Lancelot sold the castle's contents. His grandson and heir, James, inherited in 1953. James Lowther saw the house, and the wealth and splendour it exemplified, as an embarrassment. He also faced a crippling £25 million in death duties. His attempts to give the house to an official body or the National Trust were unsuccessful. This was the post-war period, and the Lowthers joined thousands of aristocratic families (many of whom had suffered devastating personal losses during the war) facing insurmountable inheritance tax and vast country piles they could no longer support. So, just 140 years after its completion, Lowther Castle was partially demolished. Its roof and all interiors were stripped, leaving nothing but the façade and outer walls. It would never be inhabited again. The gardens fell into decay and were gradually covered in

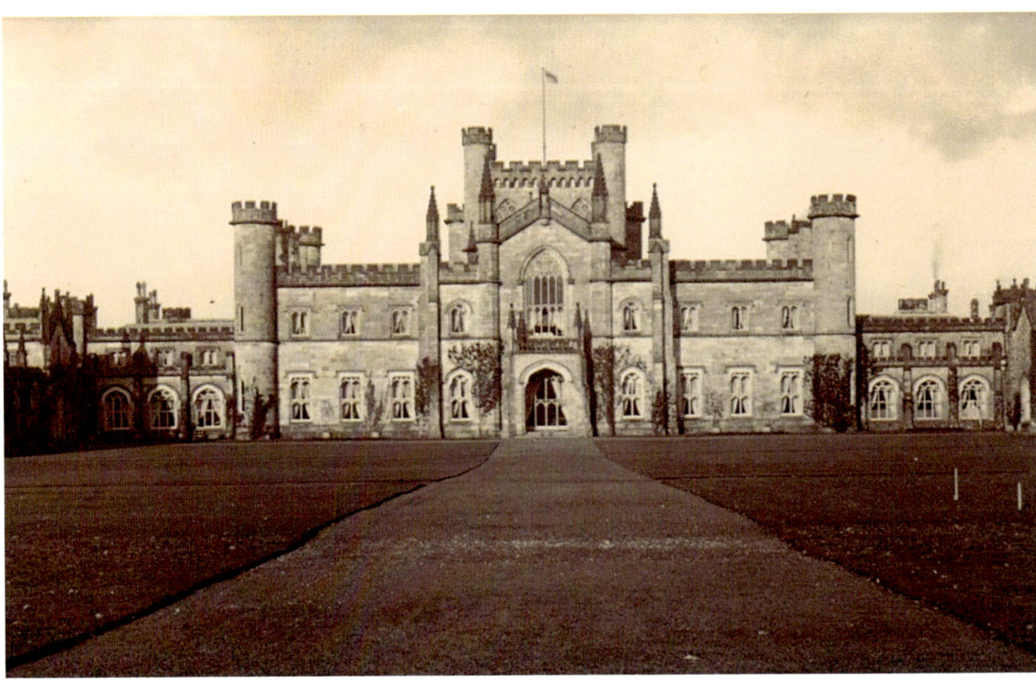

The garden front of Lowther Castle.

commercial timber, and the stables became a pig farm. The castle fell into disrepair and was abandoned for fifty years.

Over the past fifteen years, however, Lowther Castle has entered a new phase in its history. Led by the current generation of the Lowther family, the remains of the castle have been stabilised, the gardens brought back to life, and visitors are admitted all year round to walk among the ruins.

In fact, Lowther Castle isn't as big as it looks from a distance, although it is big enough for some of its more far-flung rooms to have been nicknamed Van Diemen's land. The entrance front is built in the castellated manner of Smirke's Eastnor Castle and commands a battlemented approached via ramps and a dramatic gatehouse. The central porte-cochere is flanked by the library and breakfast room and dominated by the staircase tower. Lower recessed wings contained family rooms and the dramatic façade then breaks forward, partially shielding the stables and service rooms.

The garden front is more ecclesiastical, the centre dominated by a large traceried window – the impression is much less of shifting masses than the entrance front. Sculpture galleries form what is effectively an open courtyard outside the state rooms, which are dominated by the central vast saloon and overlook the gardens. The stable court forms an open U shape to the east of the house and survives largely intact, lacking only its monumental riding house. It was here, every morning, that the Lonsdale coat of arms would be laid out in coloured chalks for the earl's dogs to scatter. Little remains of the once vast service wing.

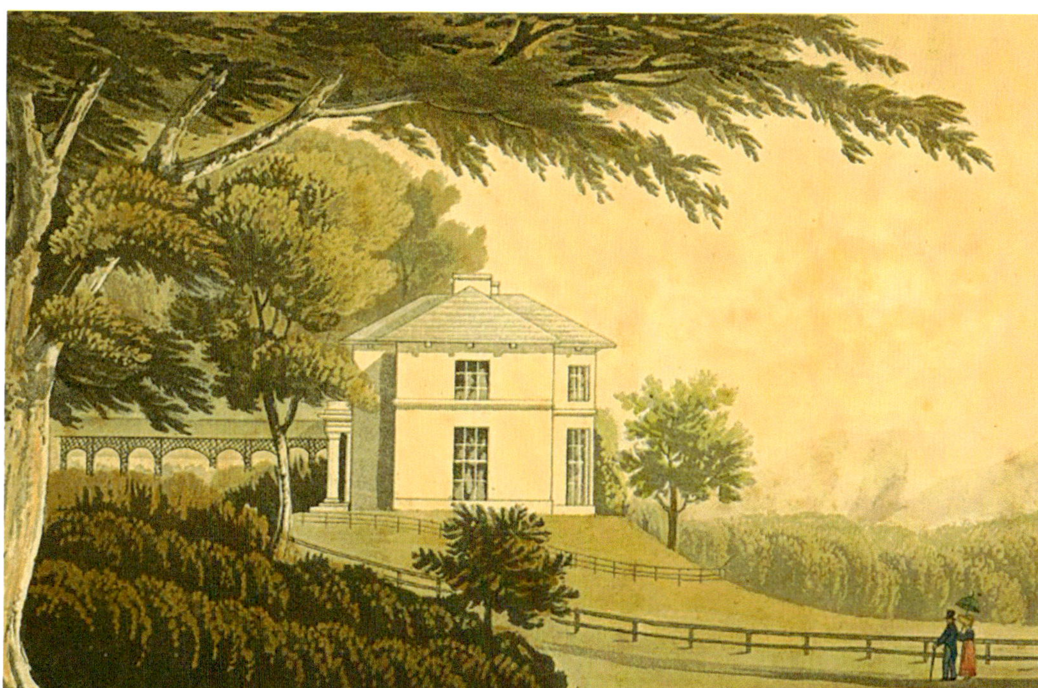

Roger Carus' House, Lunefield.

The gardens are on a princely scale and are now being restored and reinterpreted, the absence (and unaffordability) of the Yellow Earl's army of gardeners limiting the restoration of the setting at its grandest. A monumental terrace runs along and above the river valley commanding splendid views and nearby, rising above the river, is Lowther Church. Its churchyard is dominated by Benjamin Baud's 1857 mausoleum for the 2nd Earl of Lonsdale, delightfully described in Pevsner as a 'monsterpiece'. The church contains one of country's best sequences of monuments: 400 years of recumbent Lowthers. Between castle and church are the remains of the Lowther's original motte-and-bailey castle. On the other side of the park is Lowther village, an incomplete design by the Adam brothers of the 1760s. Dotted about are gate piers surviving from the earlier Lowther Hall.

## Lunefield, Kirkby Lonsdale

Roger Carus bought the Lunefield estate in 1812 and built a small classical villa in 1815. Alfred Harris, a banker, bought the estate in 1869, demolished the original house and commissioned Alfred Waterhouse to build a new mansion. In 1882 William Morris and Company supplied stained glass to the designs of Edward Burne-Jones, depicting Lancelot and Elaine. The estate was sold and broken up at the end of the nineteenth century and after use by the Army in the Second World War the house was demolished in 1958.

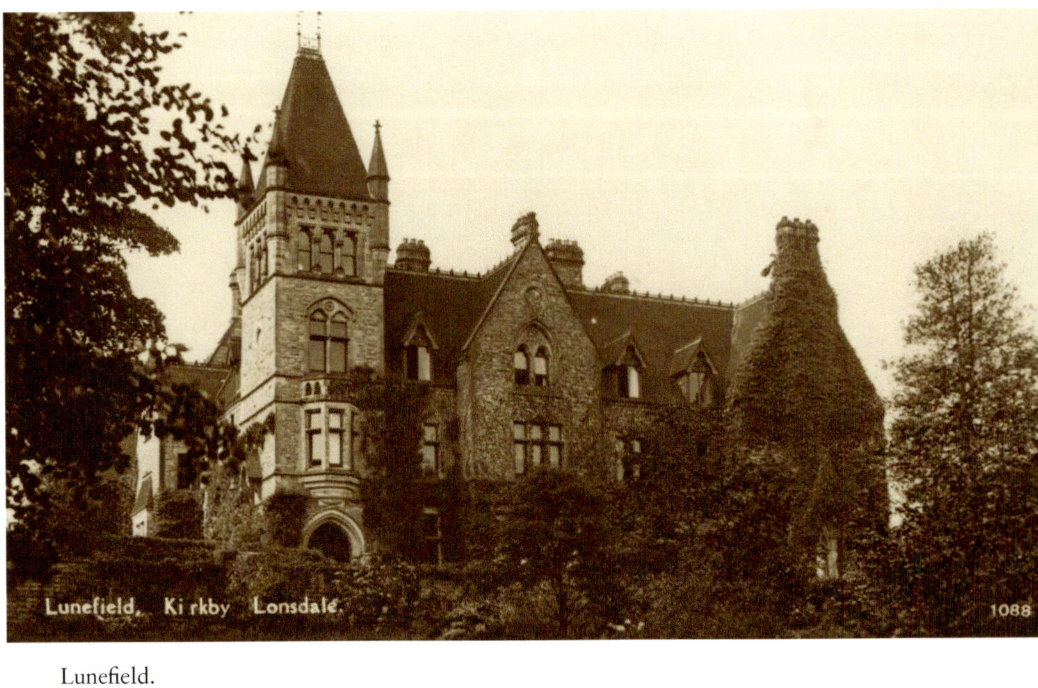


Lunefield.

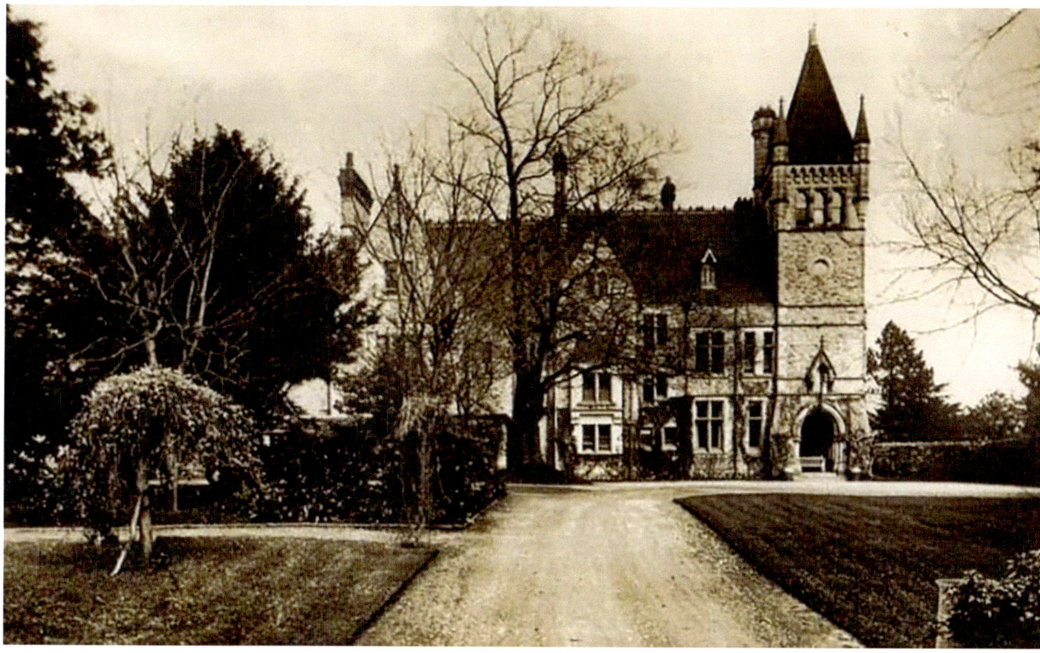

Lunefield.

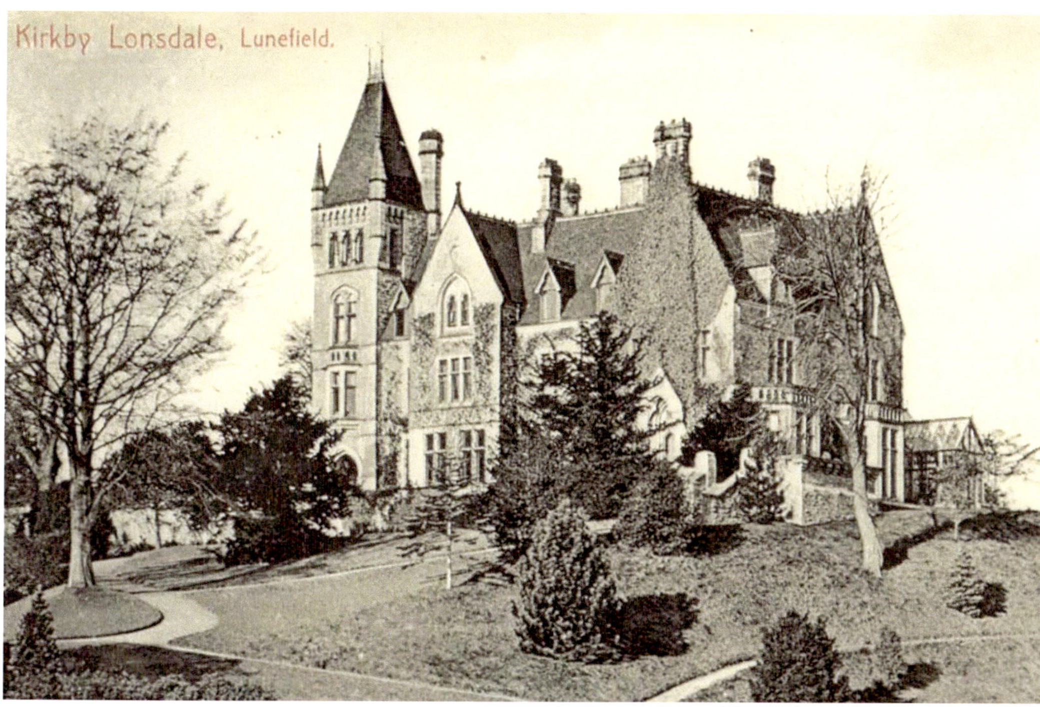


Lunefield.

## Meaburn Hall (Maulds Meaburn Hall), Maulds Meaburn

Originally a seat of the Vernon family, Sir John Lowther acquired Maulds Meaburn in 1602 and it remains part of the Lowther estate of the earls of Lonsdale. What remains was a Lowther home until the eighteenth century when half of it was demolished and the surviving fragment became a farmhouse. The main block dated from the late sixteenth century, the south wing was dated 1610 and a new staircase was inserted in 1676. Elements of a formal garden survive. It was at Maulds Meaburn that 'Wicked Jimmy', 1st Earl of Lonsdale, kept the body of his lover, the beautiful daughter of one of his tenant farmers, in a glass lidded coffin so that he could continue to admire her beauty even after her death.

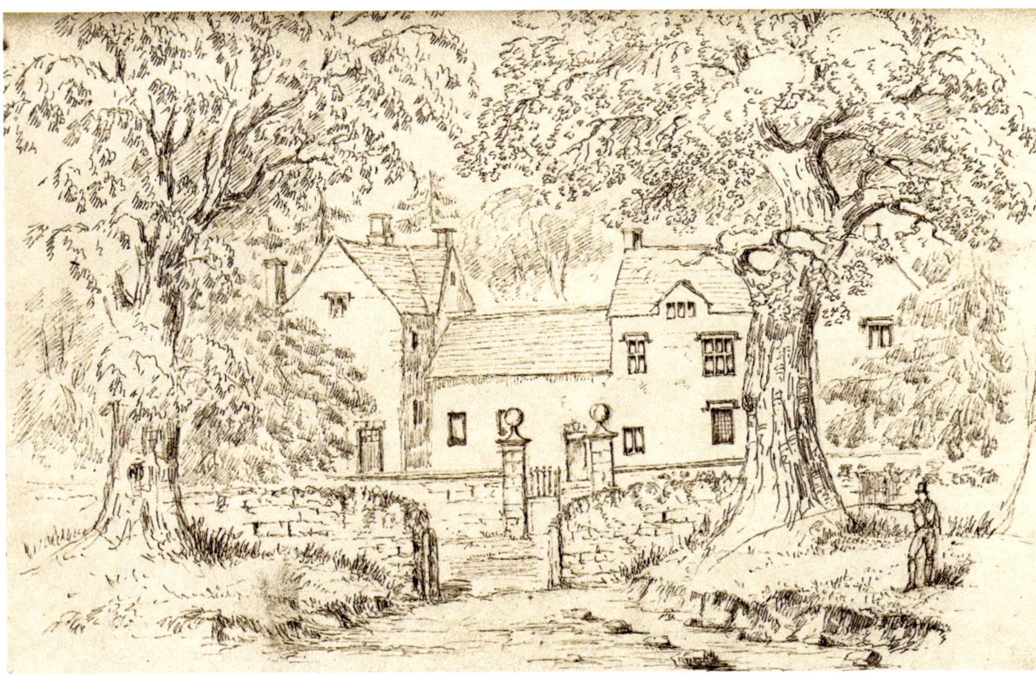

Maulds Meaburn around 1850.

## Middleton Hall, Middleton

A once substantial medieval house, Middleton Hall fell into ruin in the eighteenth century. Originally built on an H plan in the fourteenth century, the cross wings were lengthened and a curtain wall and gate house added in the fifteenth century. The hall was extended and the hall roof rebuilt in the seventeenth century and further additions made in the eighteenth and nineteenth. The screens passage with three entrances survives as does some sixteenth- and seventeenth-century panelling. A first-floor fireplace has the arms of Middleton and Middleton impaling Tunstal. The Middletons retained the estate until 1644. The remains of the hall are now a farm.

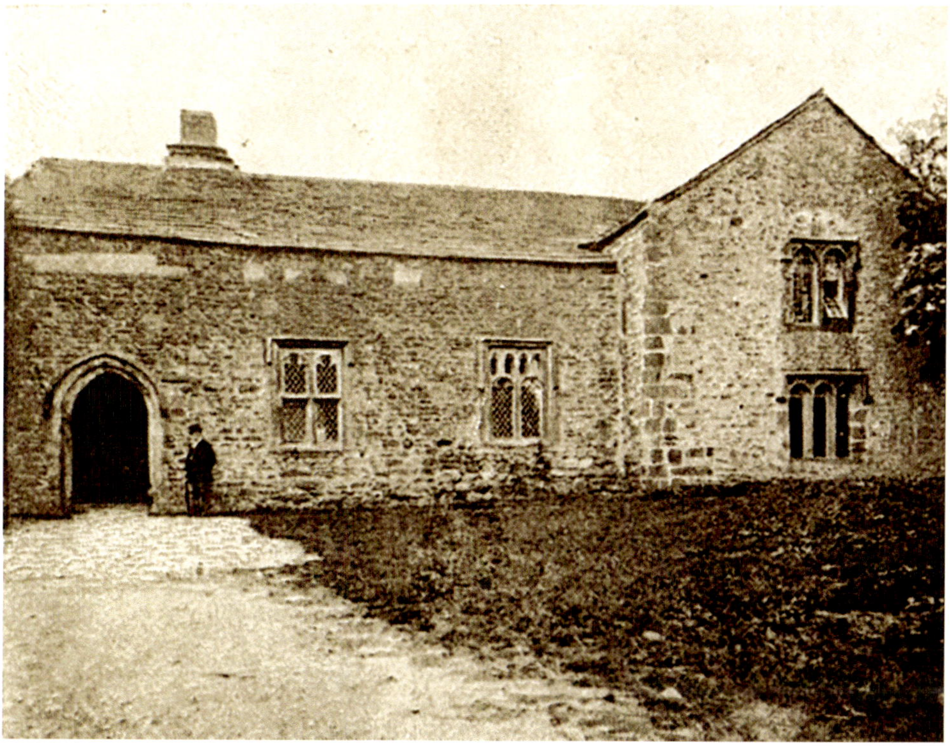

Middleton Hall.

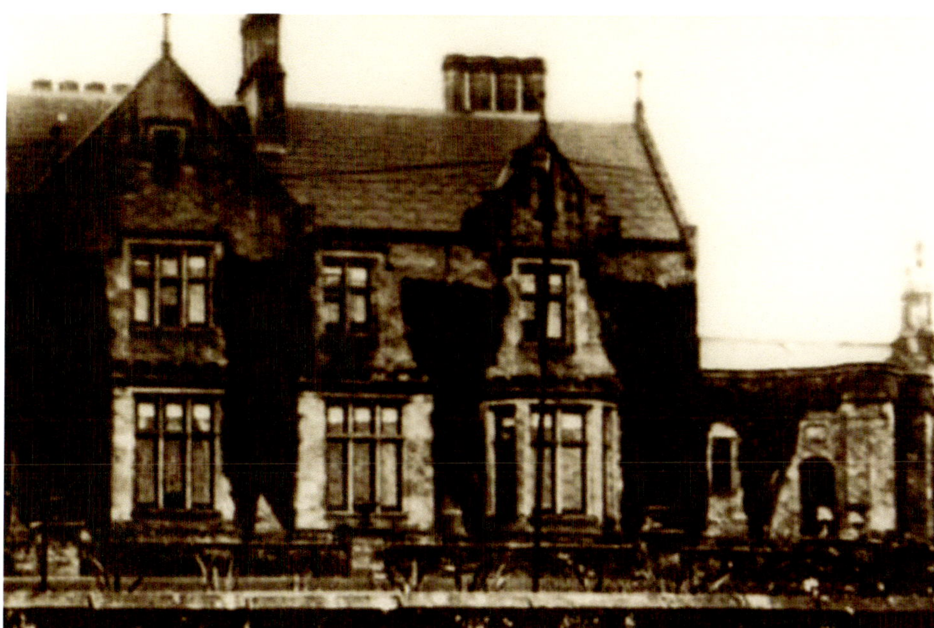

Milton Hall, Brampton.

## Milton Hall, Brampton

Probably dating from the early nineteenth century, Milton Hall later became a boarding school. The original building was largely destroyed by fire in 1960, one of the firefighters losing his life whilst fighting the fire. The school closed in 1987 and Milton Hall is now a remand home. An early nineteenth-century lodge and gate piers survive. St Marton's Church hall in Brampton was built in memory of Thomas Thompson, who owned Milton Hall and died in 1895.

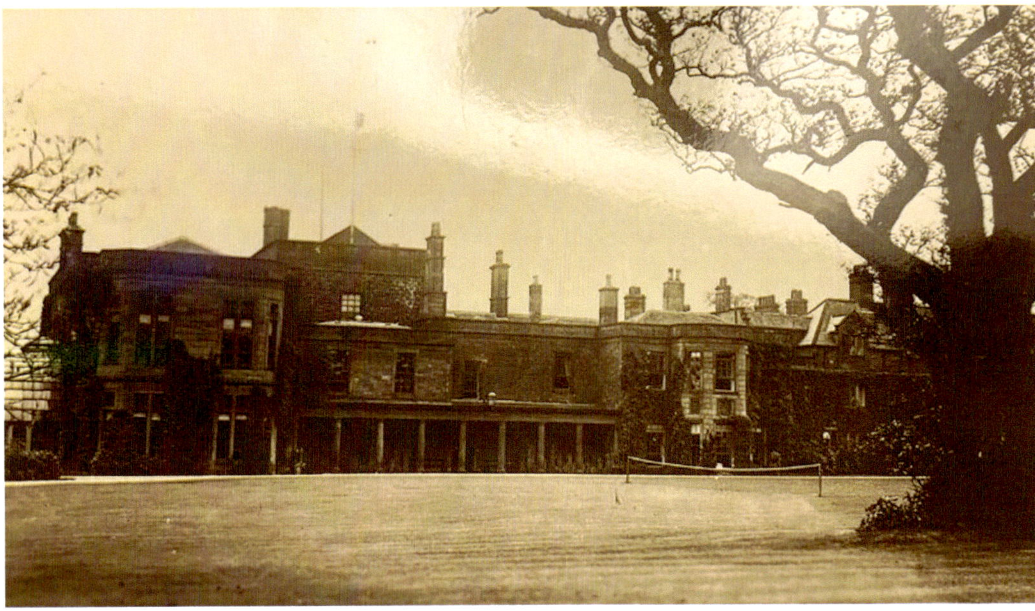

Netherhall, Maryport.

## Netherhall, Maryport

The Senhouses were the founders and leading family of Maryport and their legacy survives today in the Senhouse Museum, which contains Britain's oldest collection of Roman altars and inscribed stones. The family were pioneer collectors and preservers of Roman artifacts; they began their collection in the 1570s and displayed it at their ancestral home, Netherhall. Sadly, only a fragment remains of that seat.

The Senhouses acquired Netherhall when Elizabeth Eaglesfield married John Senhouse in the sixteenth century. John Senhouse's son, also John, was the early pioneer of the study of the Roman remains from the area and began the collection. One of the younger John's sons became Bishop of Carlisle.

In 1749 Humphrey Senhouse built a new harbour and planned town at nearby Ellenfoot, renaming it Maryport after his wife, with the aim of competing for coal shipments with the Lowthers at Whitehaven. Humphrey's son William was surveyor general of customs in Barbados where he owned and managed sugar plantations and is said, by way of recreation, to have fathered 100 children by his female slaves. In 1835 the house passed by marriage to the Pocklingtons when

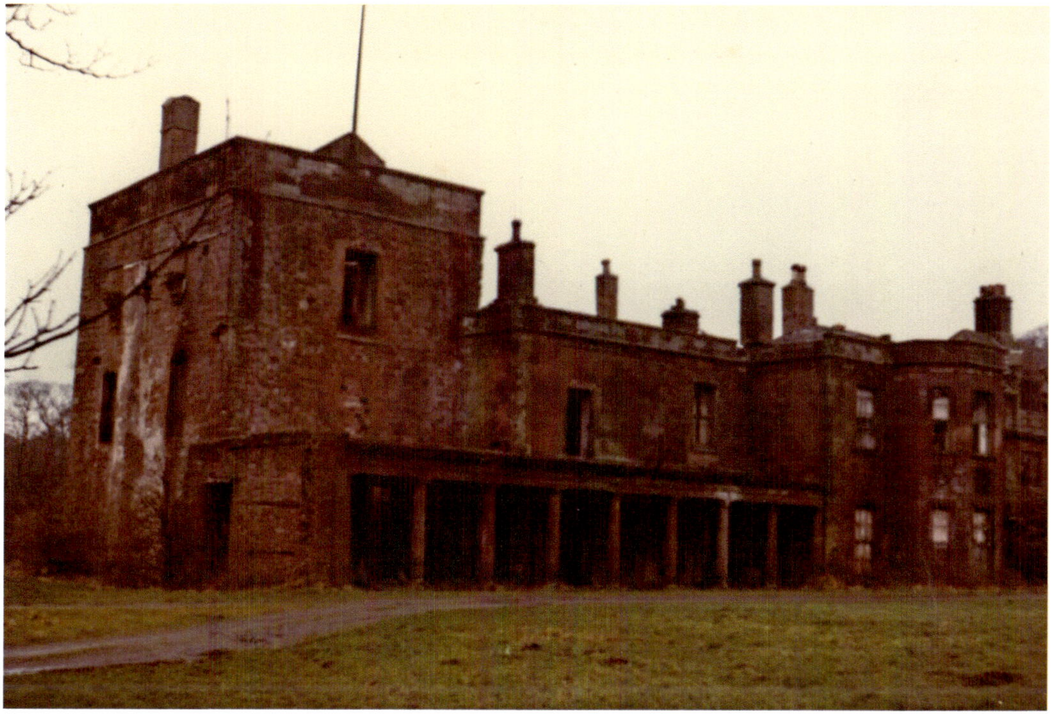

Netherhall abandoned, with the pele on the left.

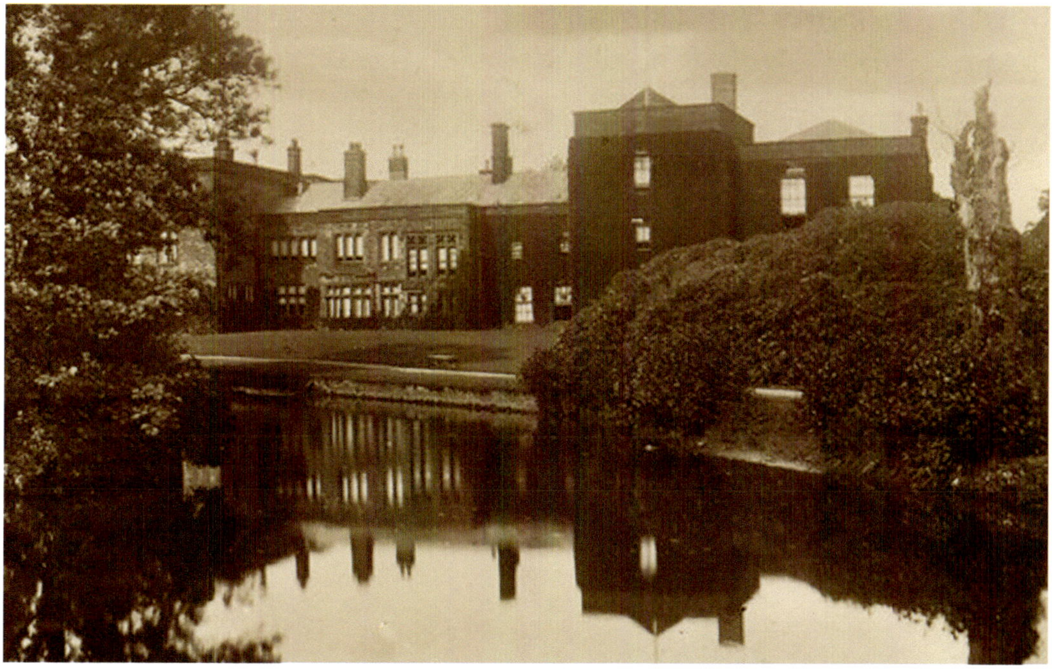

Netherhall.

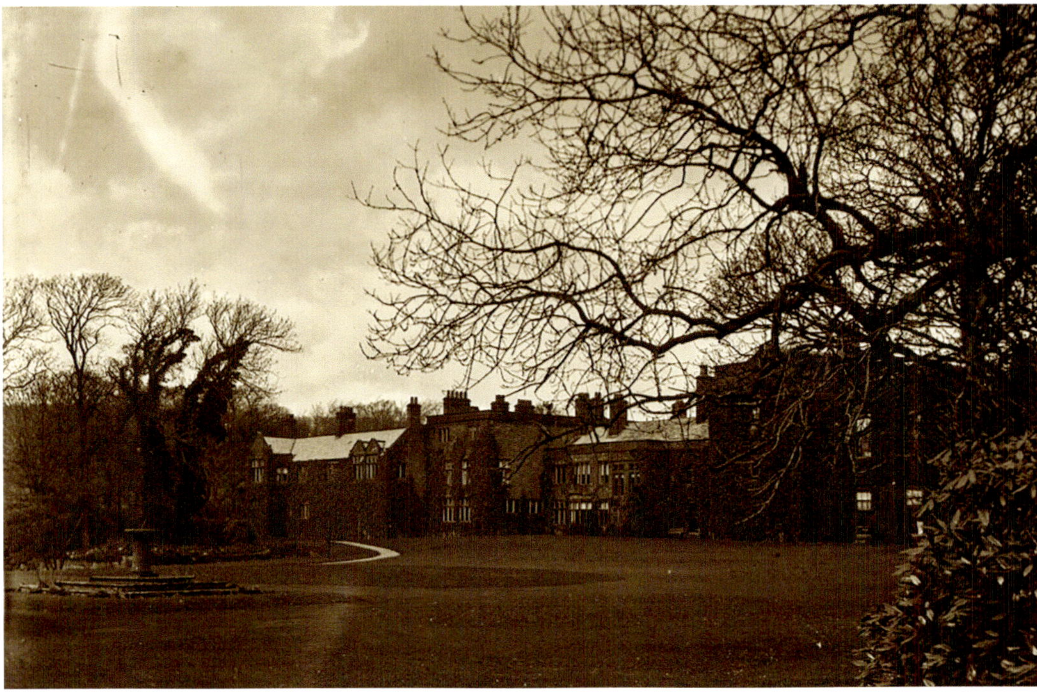

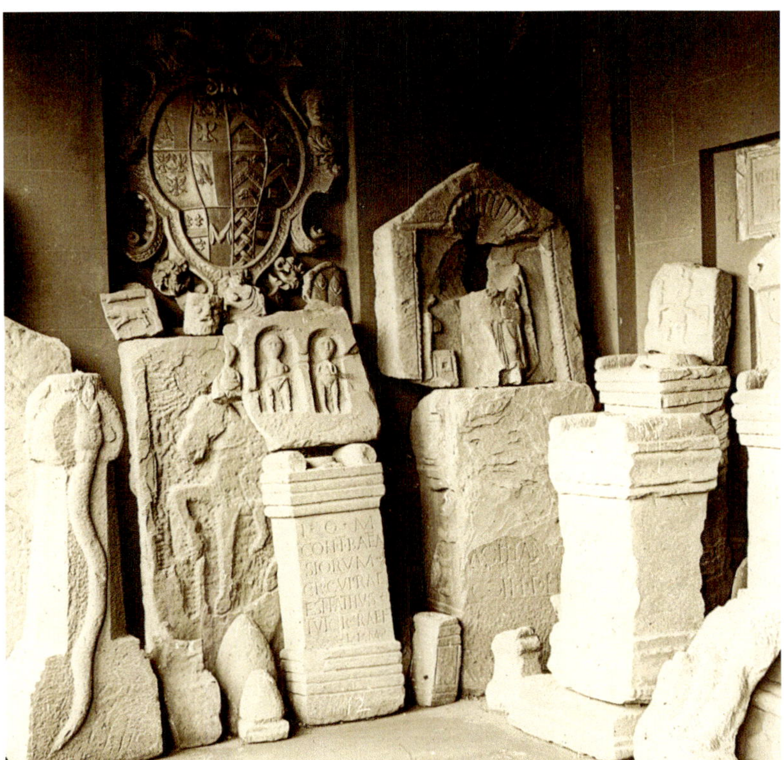

*Above*: Netherhall.

*Left*: Roman remains at Netherhall.

the heiress and philanthropist Elizabeth Senhouse married Joseph Pocklington. The Pocklingtons assumed the Senhouse name in 1842 and were the grandparents of Lord Curzon, Viceroy of India. Massive eighteenth- and nineteenth-century additions to the original pele tower transformed the mansion into a rather sprawling and shapeless mass. The hall was abandoned in the 1950s when many of the contents, including some of the Roman artifacts, were simply left in place and subject to theft and vandalism. The losses occurring at that time are unknown but what remains of the Roman stones are now safe in their own museum. The hall was demolished in 1979 after it was deliberately set on fire. The remains of an original medieval tower, ancillary buildings and a lodge with Doric columns survive. The site of the mansion and the Roman collections still belong to the descendants of the Senhouses.

## Oak Lea, Barrow-in-Furness

Designed by Paley and Austin and built in 1874 for Henry William Schneider, whose fortune came from the iron industry, Oak Lea remained empty after Scheider's death in 1887. The house was destroyed by fire in 1913. The available evidence suggested arson and female footprints were found in the ruins. Elizabeth Grew, secretary of the Barrow suffragettes, later claimed responsibility.

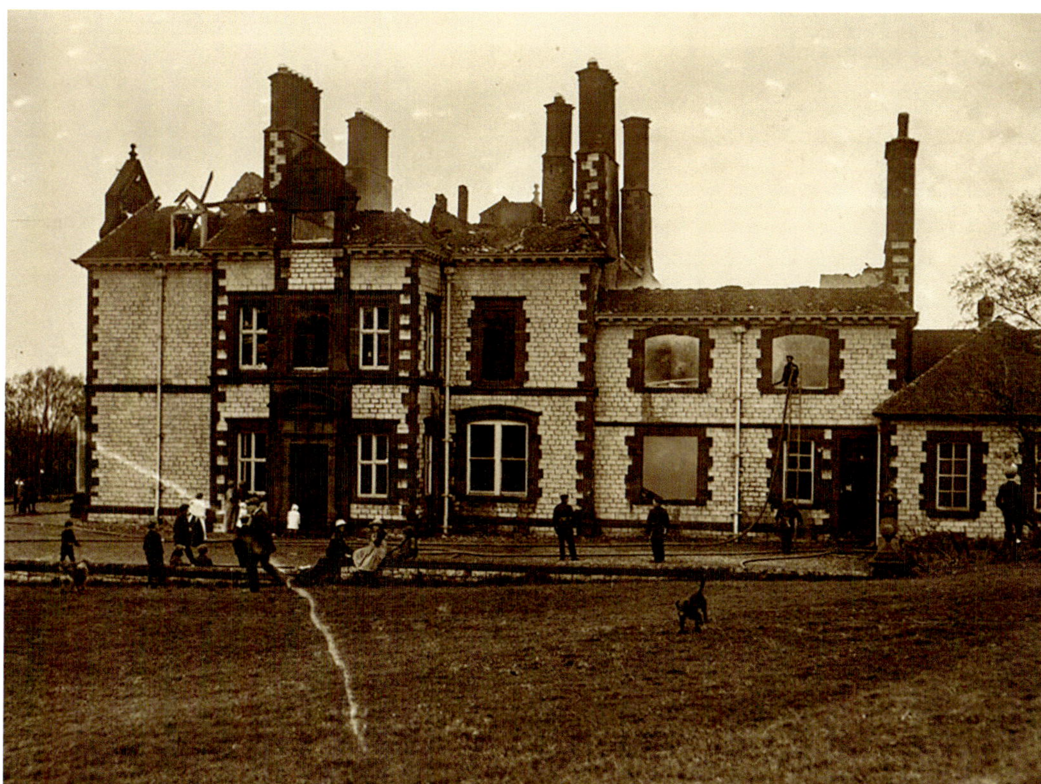

Oak Lea after the fire.

## Raw Head Hall, Raw Head

Raw Hall, ancient seat of the Sleddal(l) family, was sold to the Earl of Bective in 1871 and subsequently demolished. Bective was the son of the Irish Marquess of Headfort and served first as MP for Westmoreland and then for Kendal. He was a well-known supporter of women's suffrage. Two sets of gate piers with statues of the Sleddall greyhound and letter 'S' survive near the former school and church, suggesting a house of considerable status. In the 1880s Mannix's guide refers to 'Raw-Head, the ancient mansion of John Sleddall Esq'. John Sleddall was the founder of a set of almshouses in Kendal, built in 1887, which bear his name. His ancestor Thomas Sleddall had been Kendal's first mayor in 1636.

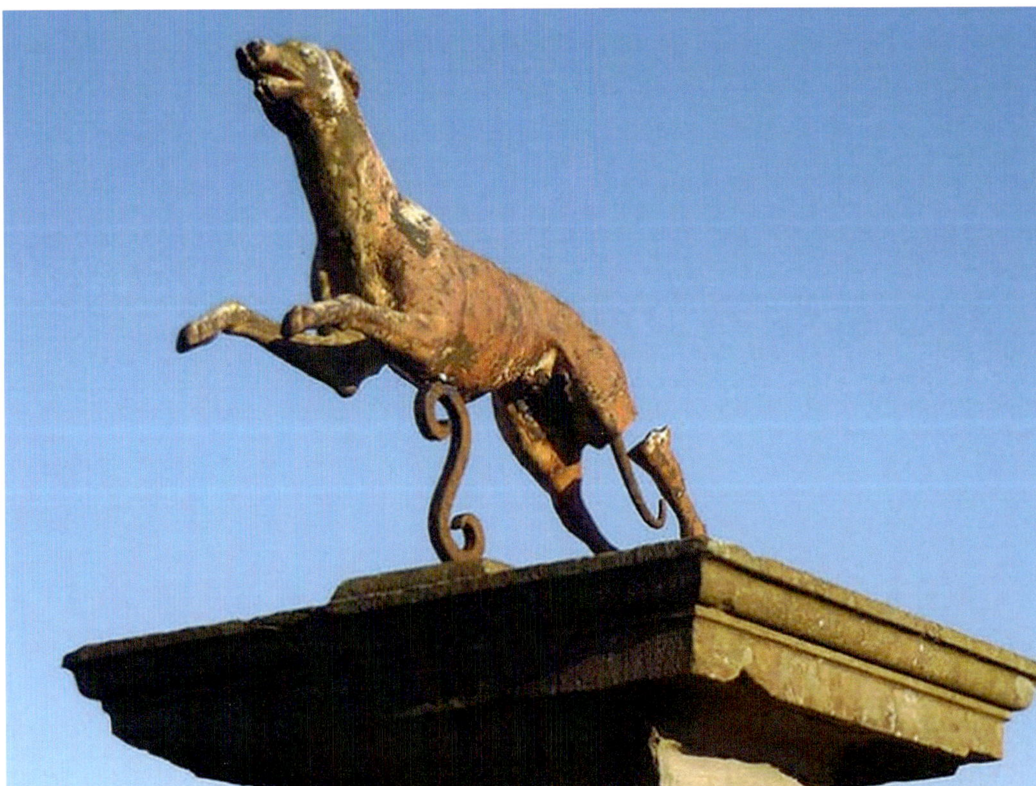

The Sleddall greyhound, Raw Head.

## Rheda Mansion, Frizington

Thomas Dixon acquired Rheda on his marriage to Mary Nicholson in 1617 and the estate remained the Dixon seat until the mid-twentieth century. The Dixons were originally yeoman farmers but became wealthy from mineral deposits underneath their land. They built a house on the site in the seventeenth century but this was replaced by a new mansion designed by Jonathan Shepherd of Whitehaven between 1881 and 1883, which was altered by Martindale of Carlisle between 1900 and 1906. The office court in Tudor style, which includes a replica

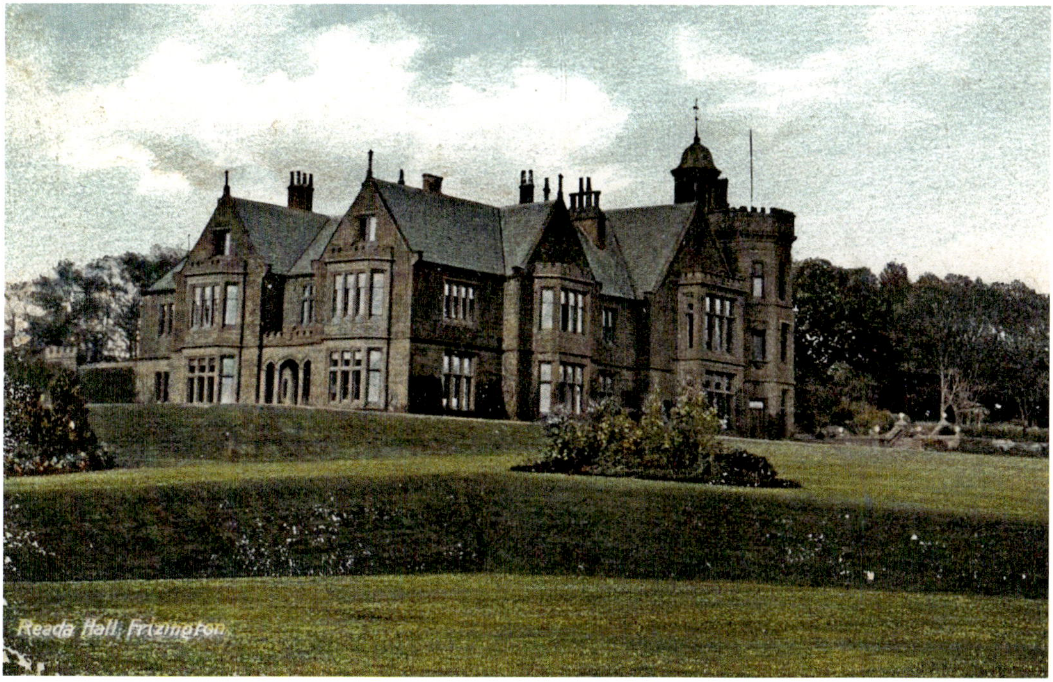


Rheda.

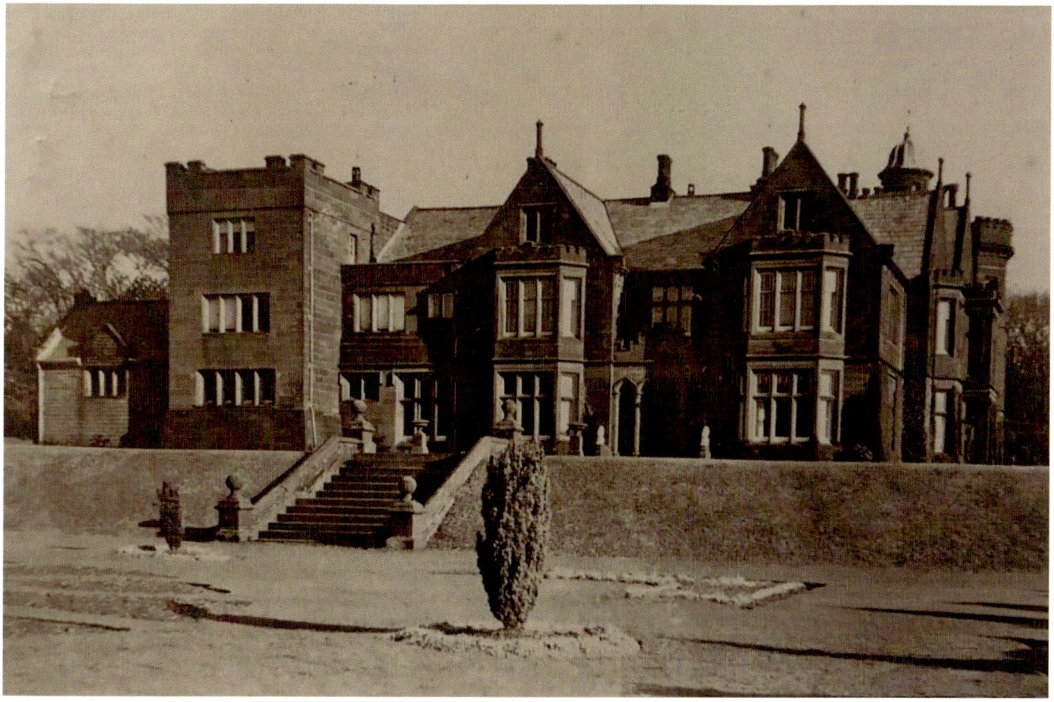

Rheda.

of a pele tower and was built in 1887 to the designs of C. J. Ferguson, survives. When Thomas Dixon died in 1922, Rheda passed to his daughter, Mrs Myfanwy Holman. Her husband was Alwyn Holman, a London lawyer whose brother, Leigh Holman, was married to the actress Vivien Leigh. Vivien Leigh was a frequent visitor to Rheda.

## Ribton Hall, Camerton

The eponymous Ribtons sold their seat to Thomas Lamplugh in the early seventeenth century. His son Richard, MP for Cumberland, built a new and rather distinguished house, probably to the designs of Edward Addison. Seven bays by three and three storeys, the entrance front was faced in stone, the sides and probably the rear rendered. The Lamplughs sold Ribton in 1722 and after long use as a farmhouse, it was demolished.

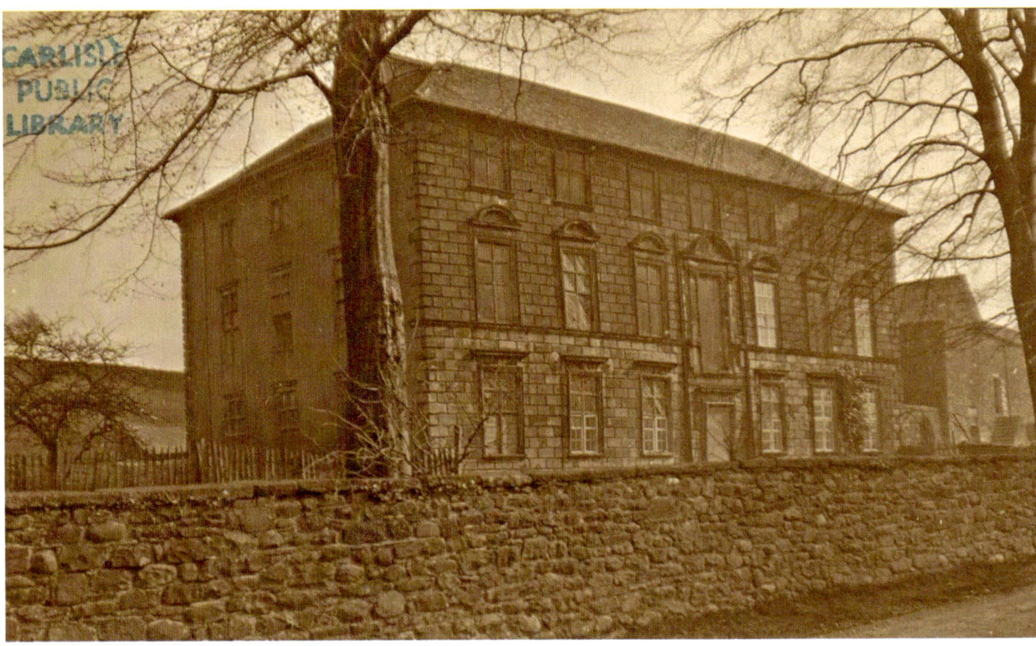


Ribton Hall.

## Summer Grove, Hensingham

Summer Grove house was of seventeenth-century origin and altered and extended in the nineteenth century. In 1761 James Spedding, the son of Carlisle Spedding, a mining engineer and agent to Sir James Lowther, bought Summer Grove from Anthony Grayson. When Spedding's great-grandson died unmarried in Capri in 1924, Summer Grove passed to his cousin Mark Quayle. In 1931 the estate was sold to Quayle's relative John Anthony Spedding of Keswick. The Speddings are now seated at Mirehouse on Bassenthwaite Lake. A Gothic arched entrance which once led to the house survives but halls of residence for the University of Central Lancashire have been built on the site.

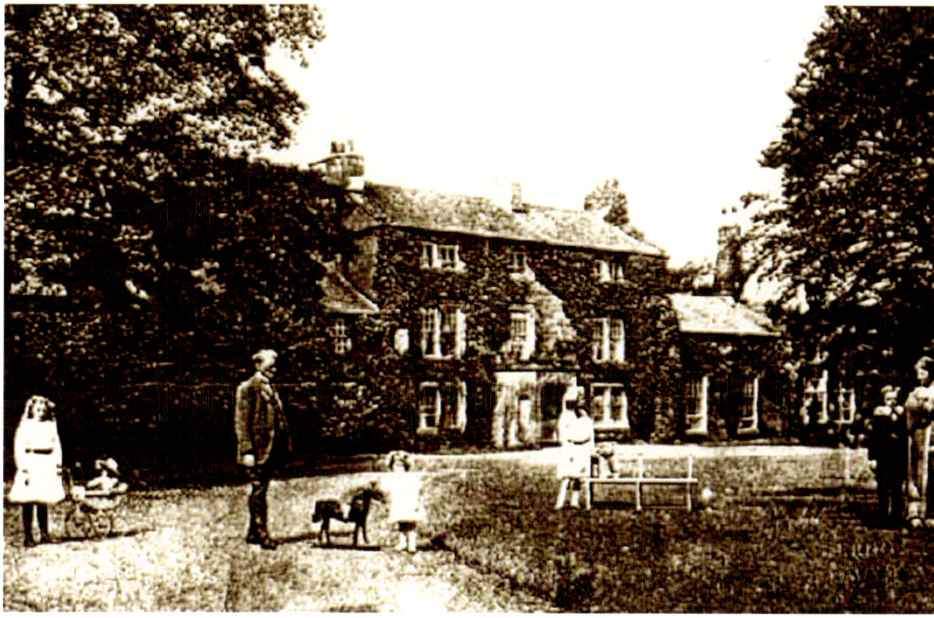

Summer Grove.

## Warwick Hall, Warwick

Originally the seat of the recusant Warwick family, their ancient hall was largely rebuilt in 1828. This hall was destroyed by fire in 1933 but once again rebuilt. Colonel Guy Elves's new house is in a loose neoclassical style, unlike anything else in the county, Poirot-esque with pilasters, lots of glass and a copper cupula over the stairs. Warwick Hall remained in the Elwes family until Mrs Aileen Elwes died in 1996. Val Marriner and her husband bought the estate in 1998 and it is now run as a bed and breakfast business. The stables and lodge of the earlier house survive.

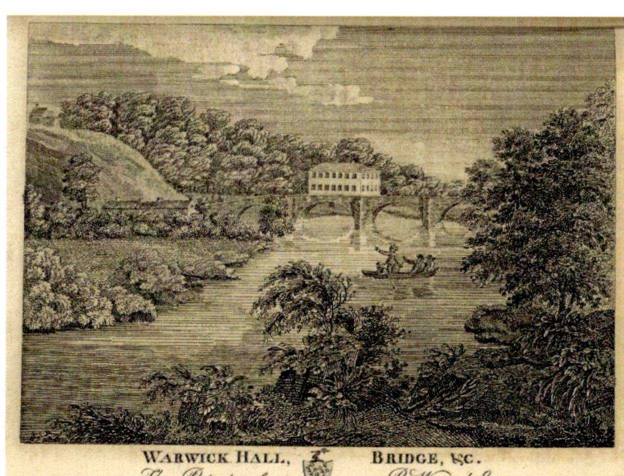


Warwick Hall, 1794.

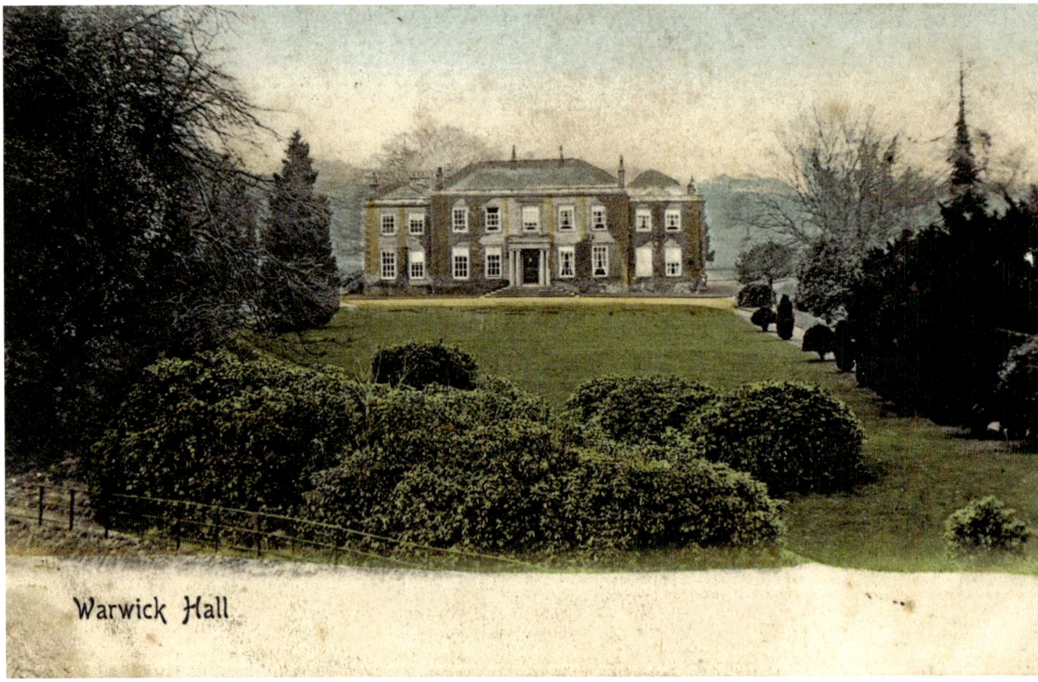


Warwick Hall.

## Wharton Hall, Kirkby Stephen

Of early fifteenth-century origin, the house of the Whartons survives as a ruin. In its original form it consisted of a great hall with a pele tower at one end and service rooms at the other, together with a freestanding kitchen. During the Pilgrimage of Grace in 1536 the manor was besieged by the forces of the rebel Robert Aske. The hall was greatly enlarged by Thomas, 1st Lord Wharton, around the time he had been elevated to the peerage in 1542 following his spectacular victory against the Scots at the Battle of Solway Moss. His arms with the date 1559 appear on the gatehouse. Amongst Wharton's additions was a grand banqueting hall, fragments of which, with the remains of the kitchen and service rooms, survive. In 1559 Wharton added another range, containing a gallery, as well as a set of apartments known as the priest's lodgings and a new gatehouse. In order to create a new park, the nearby village of Wharton was moved away from the hall. The scale of Wharton's architectural modifications reflected his political ascendency; his elevation to the nobility required a family seat of suitable magnificence. The hall would later host royalty: Mary Queen of Scots stopped at Wharton on her way from Lowther Castle to Bolton Castle in 1568 and fifty years later her son James I and VI visited when returning from Scotland.

The castle was little used by the Whartons after the seventeenth century and gradually fell into disrepair. The family lost it on the exile as a Jacobite of Philip, 1st Duke of Wharton, in 1729. This Wharton was a notorious rake; now infamous for founding the first Hellfire Club, Alexander Pope described him as 'the scorn and wonder of our days'. Robert Lowther bought Wharton Hall in 1728. In 1785,

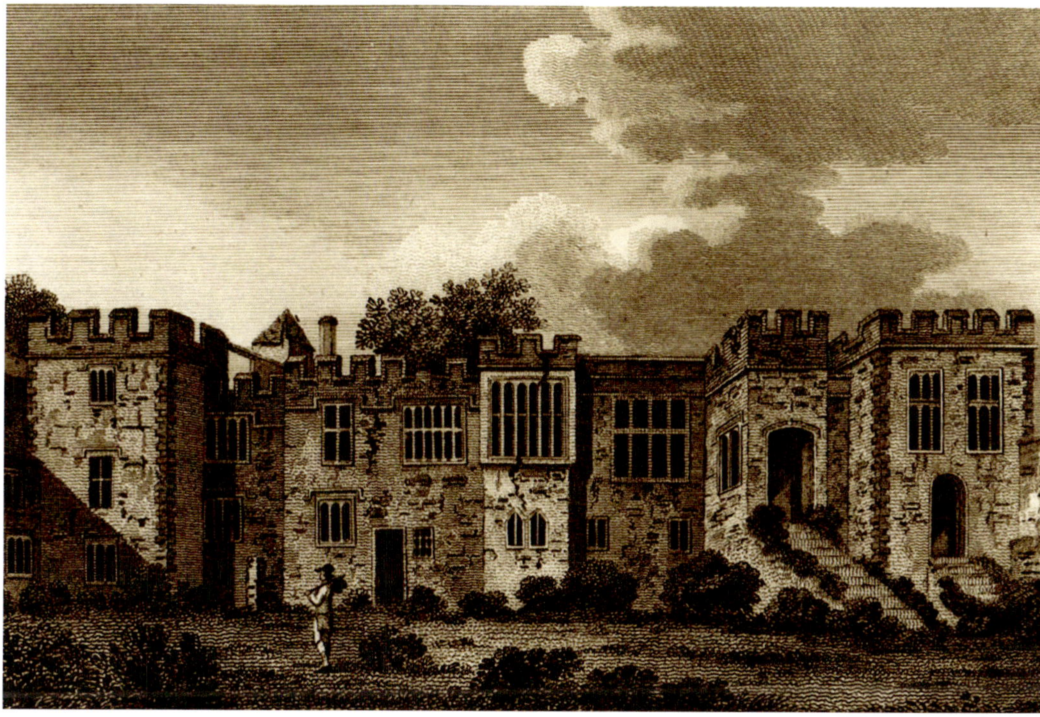

Wharton Hall in 1773.

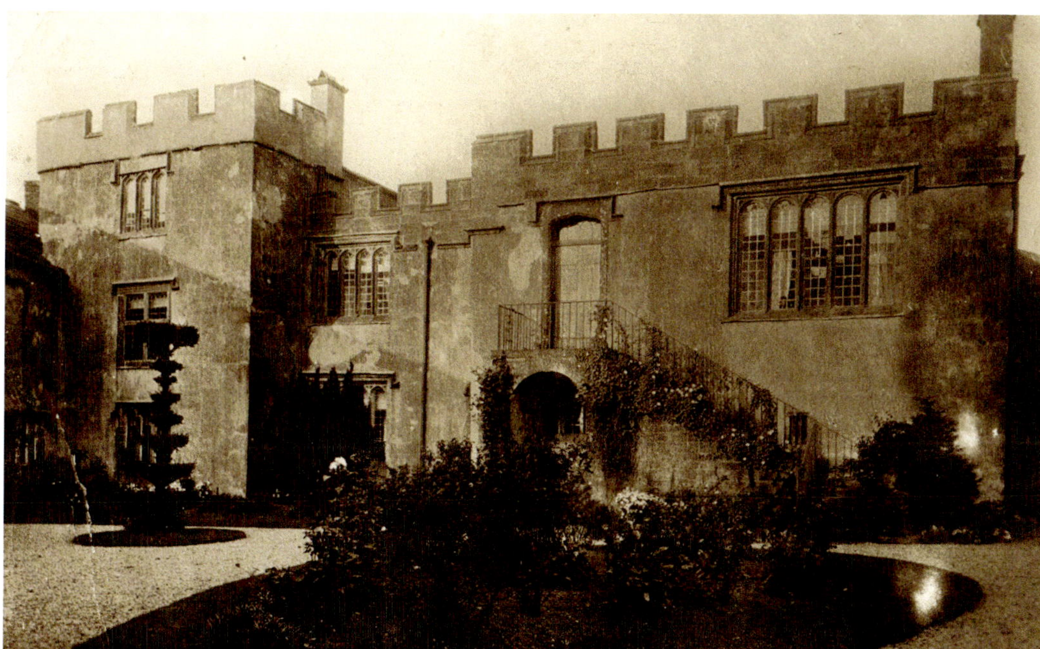

Wharton Hall.

the Earl of Lonsdale restored the castle for use as a farm, it having been described eight years previously as 'in ruins and desolate, inhabited by no human creature but a poor hind'. Further restoration took place in the twentieth century.

## Whitehall, All Hallows (Mealsgate)

George Moore was born into a family of Cumbrian statesmen, or yeoman farmers, in 1806. Apprenticed to a draper and fiercely ambitious, in 1827 he became a travelling salesman for a London firm establishing such a reputation that he became known as the 'Napoleon of Watling Street'. Aged twenty-three, he became a partner in Groucock, Copestake & Moore and eventually became very wealthy. Retiring from business on the grounds of ill health, he devoted himself to philanthropy, donating large sums of money to, amongst many others, the British Home for Incurables, the Porters' Benevolent Association and the Royal Free Hospital. In later life Moore moved from his mansion in Kensington Palace Gardens to his Cumbrian home, buying Whitehall and commissioning Antony Salvin in 1862 to extend it in his 'Tudor' manner incorporating the pele tower of the Salkelds, owners of the estate from the fourteenth century to 1746, after which the hall had gradually fallen into decay. The pele tower, which survives, has the inscription 'Lancelotus Salkeld Filius Thomae Salkeld Hoc Fieri Fecit 1589'.

Moore died in 1876, having been hit by a runaway horse. He had no children and the estate passed to his kin the Parkin-Moores, descendants of his sister Mary. The ground floor of the hall has a fireplace dated 1900 and inscribed 'W. & L. P.M.' (Parkin-Moore). Whitehall was sold to the county council after the Second

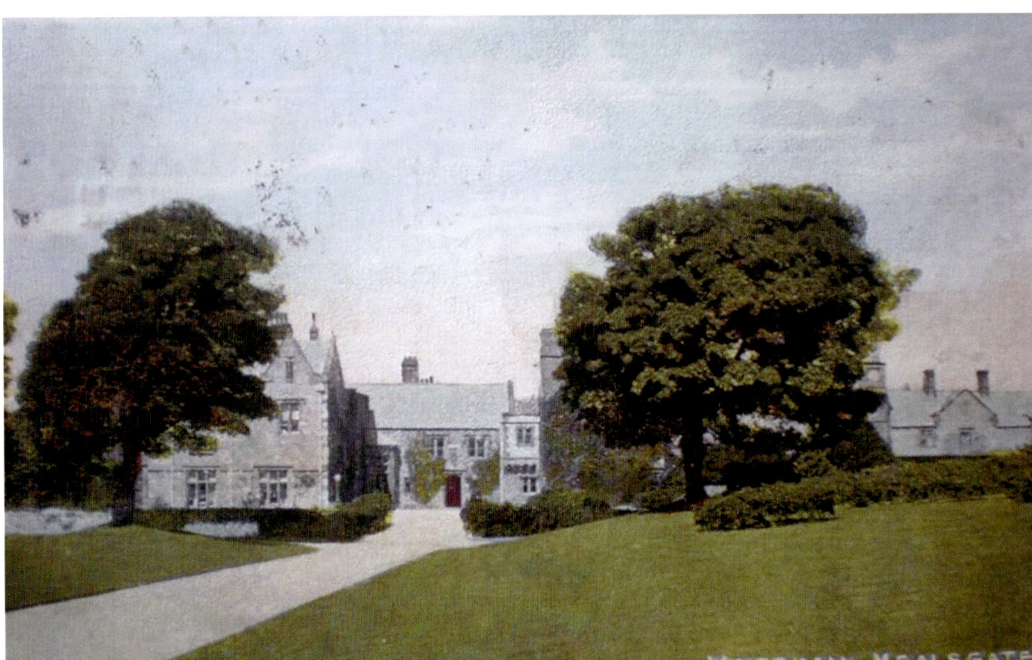


Whitehall, All Hallows.

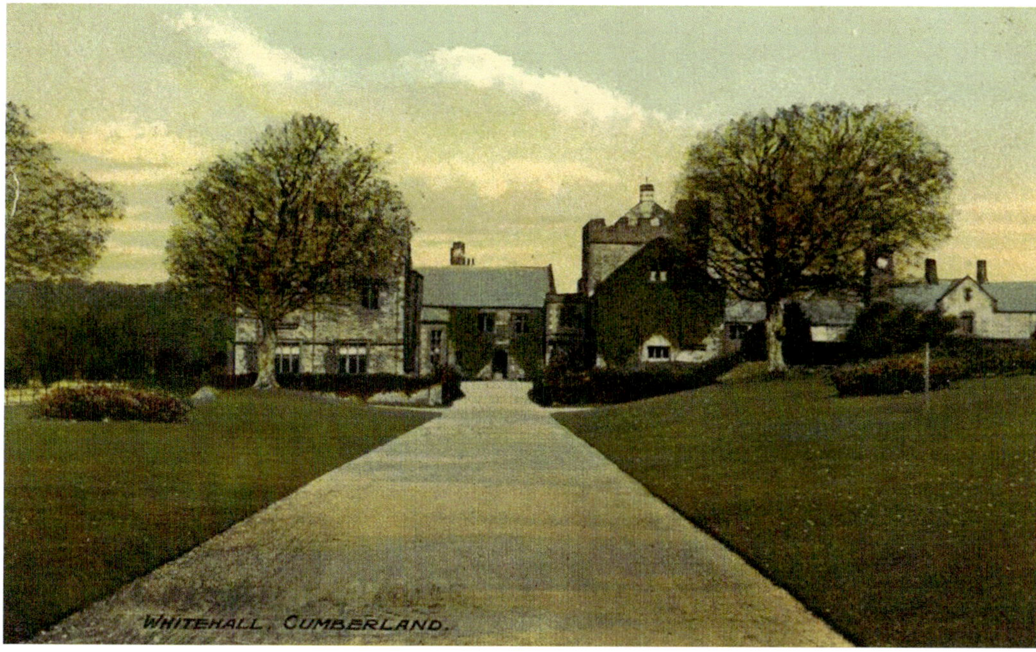


Whitehall, All Hallows.

World War and was used by the Civil Defence Corps for training in demolition techniques in the 1960s. The council later sold what was left back to the Parkin-Moore family. A small Norman chapel stands nearby and the new church has a plaque erected by the French government in honour of Moore's work during the 1871 siege of Paris when he brought food and money to its newly liberated citizens.

## Wood Hall (Woodhall), Bridekirk

William Grisdale, a local boy who became wealthy as a London brewer, bought Wood Hall in 1707 from the Tolson family, who are said to have owned the estate since Saxon times. The property passed by marriage from Grisdale's daughter to the Lucock family in 1727. At some time in the eighteenth century a new hall in classical style with seven bays, the middle three under a pediment, was built. The Fisher family bought Wood Hall in the early nineteenth century.

The Georgian hall burnt down in the 1870s. The estate was bought by Edward Tyson, a local solicitor and Lord Lieutenant of Cumberland, who built another new house. Tyson commissioned Edward Mawson to design new gardens for his house. Wood Hall was demolished in 1946 as a result of extensive dry rot. Initially left to decay, subsequent owners have partially restored Mawson's garden and two summerhouses have survived. A smaller house stands on the site of the stables.

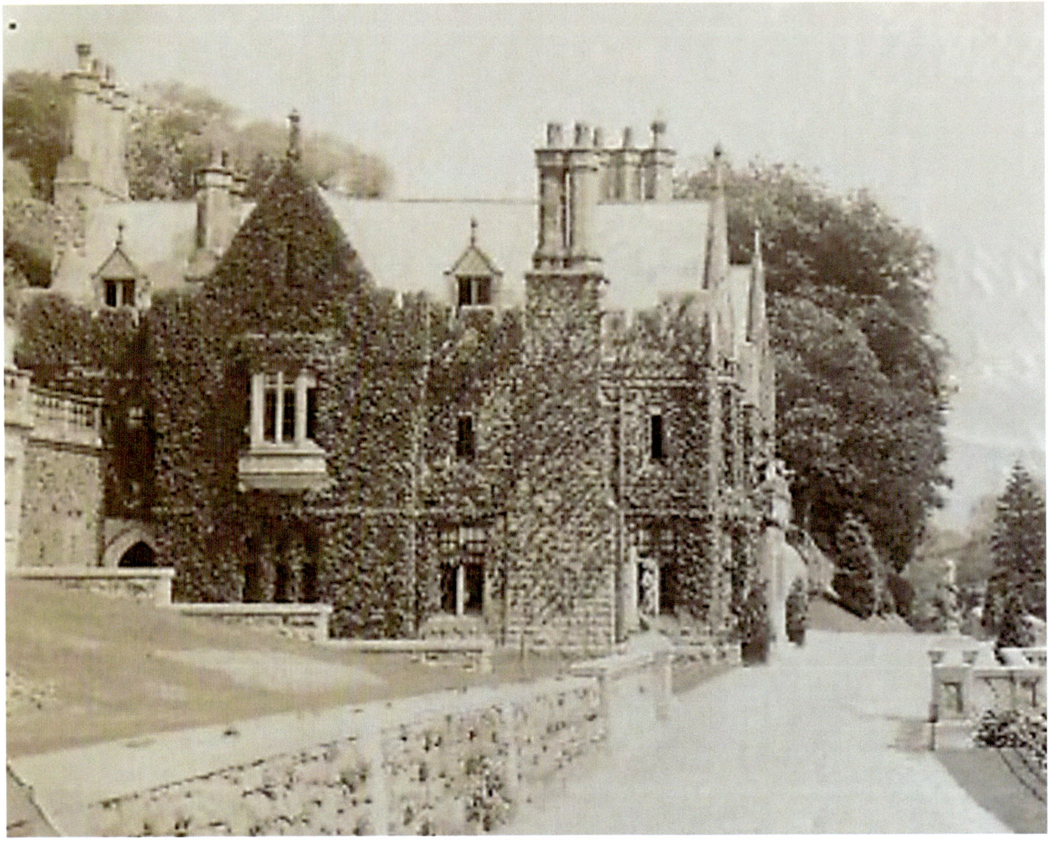

Wood Hall.

## Woodside, Wreay

The Loshes (originally Arloshes) were an ancient Cumbrian family associated with Woodside and seated there in Tudor times. The eighteenth century brought wealth from the manufacture of soda for glass making. At this time the estate was the seat of John Losh, the 'Big Black Squire', who built a neat seven-bay classical box, the three centre bays breaking forward under a pediment. There was an Ionic porch and a tall pedimented wing connected to the main block by a single-storey link. John, the builder of the new house, was succeeded by his son and on his death in 1814, his daughters Sarah and Katherine inherited the estate.

The most famous Losh of Woodside was John's daughter Sarah, subject of Jenny Uglow's biography *The Pinecone*, and builder of Wreay's astonishing Byzantine church enriched with carvings of animals, fossils and dinosaurs. Sarah's copy of the Bewcastle Cross stands nearby as a memorial to her parents. So innovative in many ways, sadly Sarah and her sister replaced their grandfather's house with a rather dull 'Tudor' building with a single two-storey bay and irregularly placed mullion and transom windows. Inside, the rooms, including a galleried hall, reflected a passion for the medieval. During the rebuilding, the remains of a pele tower were apparently identified.

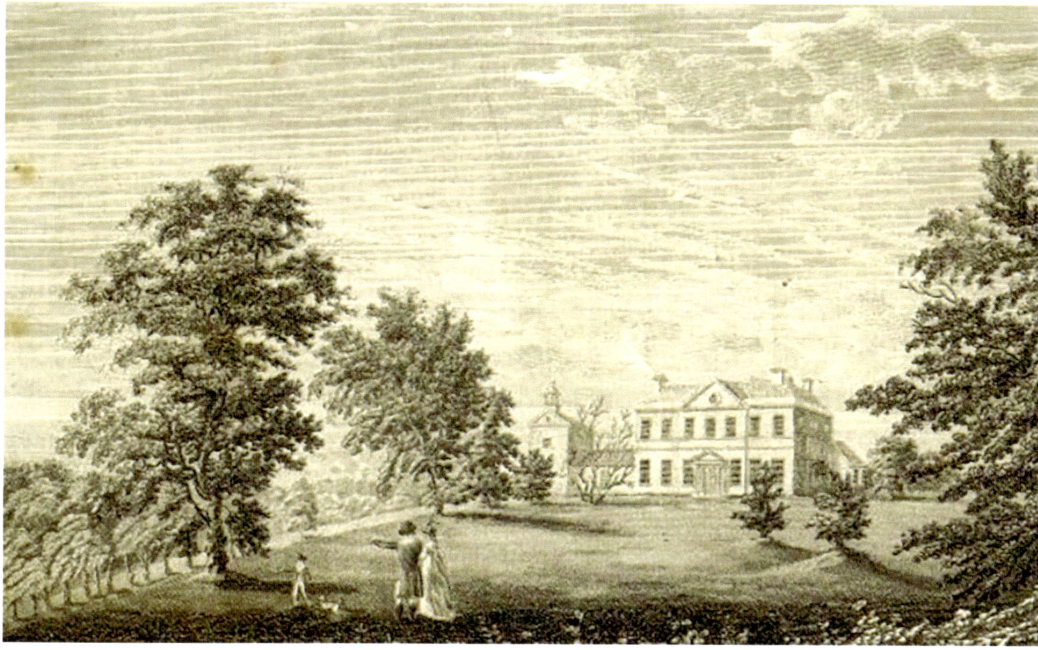

The Georgian house, Woodside.

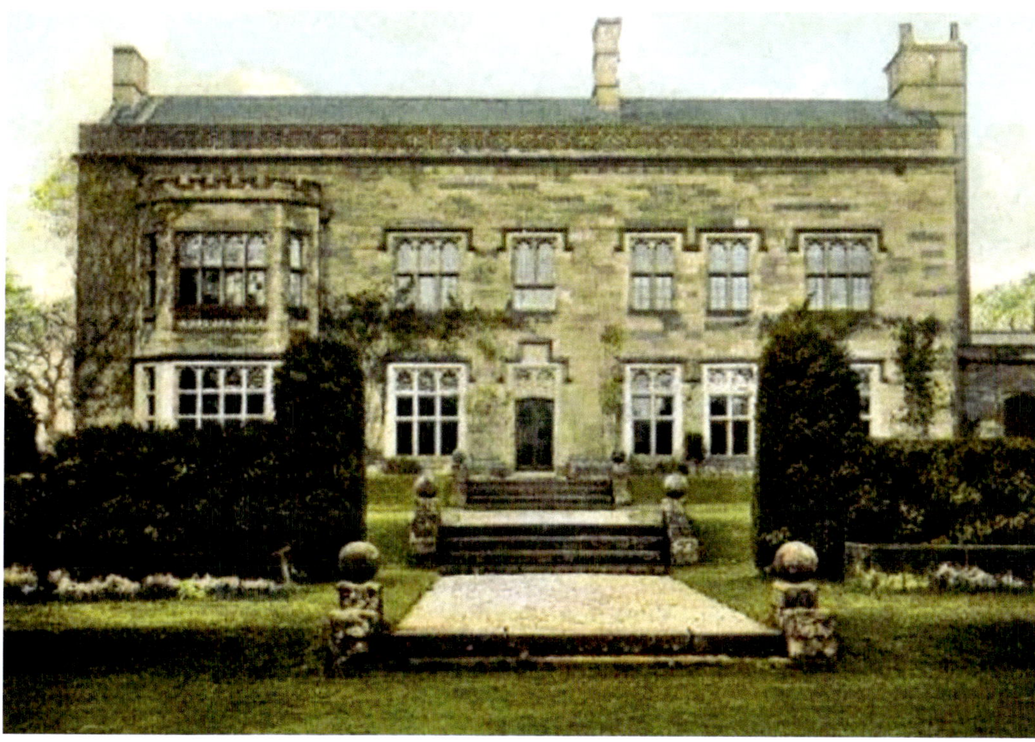

Woodside after its nineteenth-century remodelling.

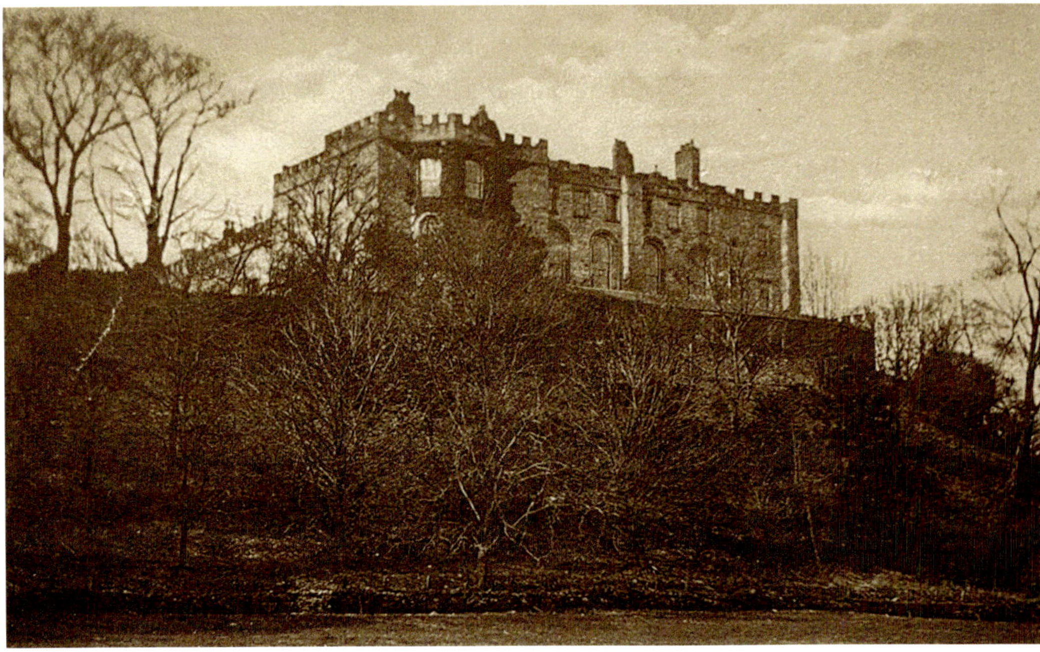

Workington Hall.

After Sarah's death in 1853, the house was inherited by her great-nephew, Unitarian clergyman James Losh (who changed his name back to Arlosh), who was still a teenager. James Arlosh's only child, Godfrey, was killed in a riding accident in 1890 when an undergraduate in Oxford and James and his wife left the area, losing interest in the estate. Dying within two weeks of each other in 1904, Woodside was left to Manchester College, a Unitarian college in Oxford. Given that there was no shortage of potential heirs, this was not a popular decision within the family. Andrew Gibson, a Liverpool shipowner, bought Woodside in 1911. Mrs Gibson died before the couple could move into Woodside, which was left deserted and fell into disrepair after the roof was removed in order to avoid paying rates. In the 1930s the property was bought by Geoffrey Carr of the Carr's biscuit factory in Carlisle, but only one wing could be saved.

## Workington Hall (Curwen Hall), Workington

Substantial consolidated ruins remain of Workington Hall, sitting outside the post-industrial town, its position high above the river indicating its original defensive purpose. But for local authority disinterest, the hall might have been an important tourist attraction, and unfortunately one of Cumberland's most historic buildings and some of its finest interiors were lost.

The oldest range of the hall stands on a cliff overlooking the River Derwent. A pele tower was built in 1362 and survives, along with the cellars of the Curwens' fourteenth-and early fifteenth-century house. The family obtained a licence to crenellate their 'house at Wyrkyngton' in 1380, presumably referring

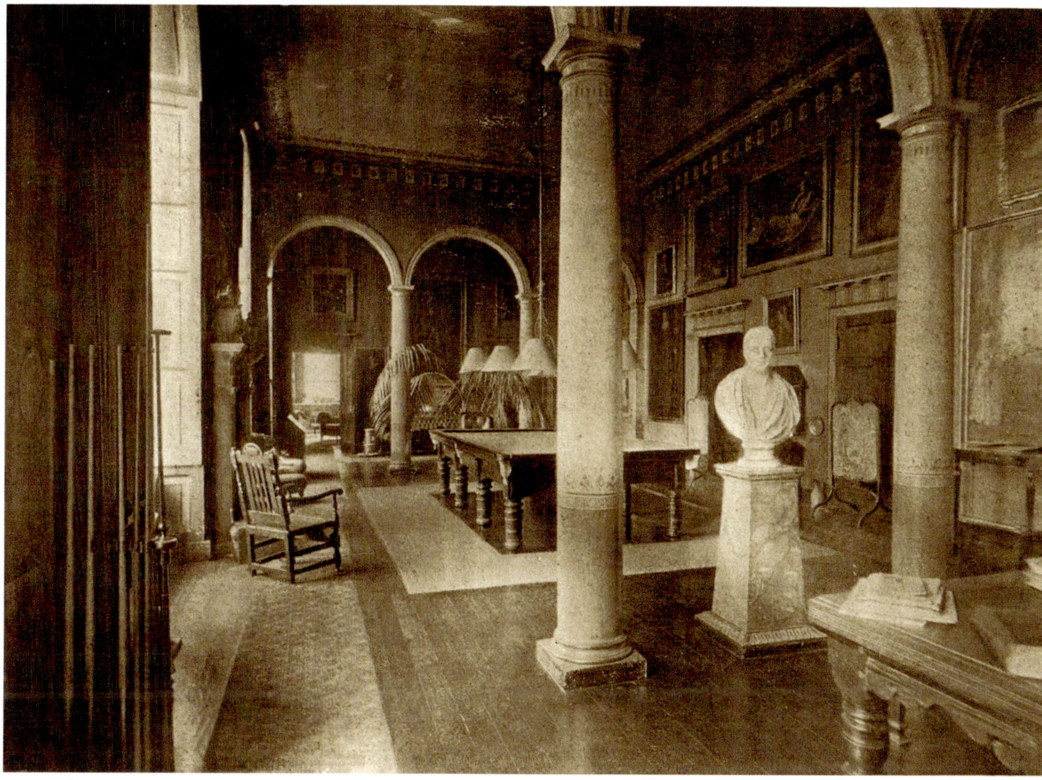

The saloon of Workington.

to the massive tower with vaulted basement, intramural passages and garderobes at the south-east corner of the later mansion. A large range to the north with a projecting diagonal corner turret was added to the tower in the fifteenth century. The Elizabethan north and south ranges connected the hall range to the gatehouse opposite. The gatehouse itself is probably fourteenth century. The antiquarian and historian William Camden described Workington in the late sixteenth century as 'a most stately castle-like feat'.

In the sixteenth century the house was witness to the border skirmishes and battles that occupied successive Tudor Curwens. In 1570s Sir Henry Curwen, after a successful foray over the border into Annandale and Galloway, returned home with iron gates he had taken from Caerlaverock Castle during a raid and proudly installed them at Workington. In May 1568 Mary Queen of Scots was an enforced but honoured guest of the Curwens.

John Carr remodelled Workington in the 1780s for John and Isabella Curwen, providing state rooms and a courtyard corridor to improve access. Large windows were added to the ancient part of the house and the original tower heightened. John Martin Robinson describes the saloon, dining room and library as having been the finest suite of classical rooms in Cumberland. Gillows provided new

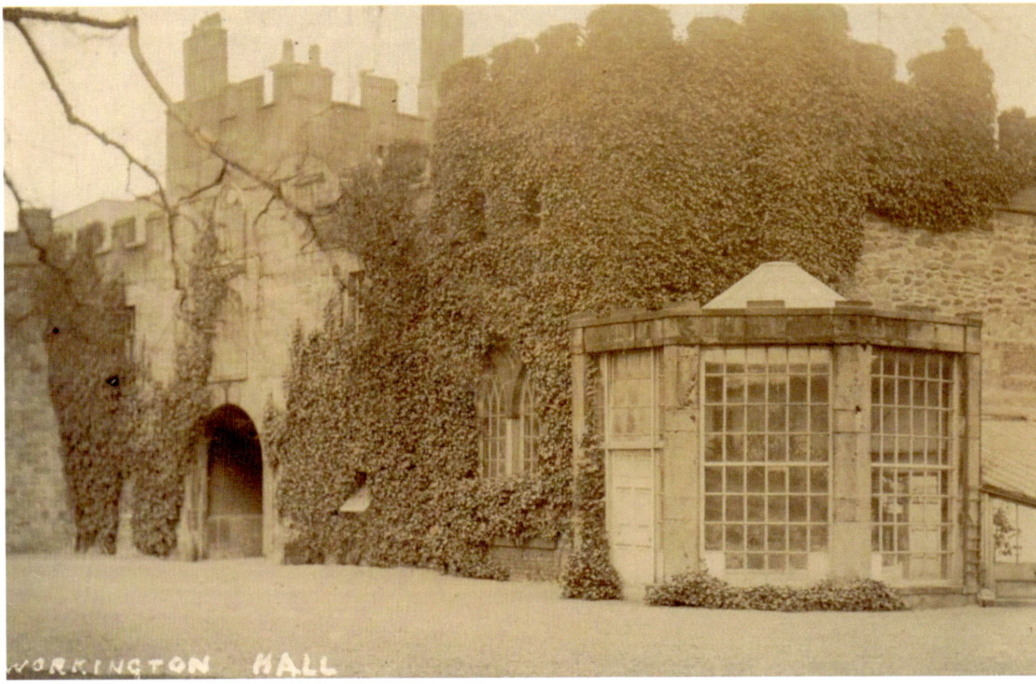


Workington Hall.

furniture and there was exceptional plasterwork. The gardens were laid out by Thomas White at around the same time.

In the early nineteenth century the property passed to John Christian Curwen, born John Christian, who married his cousin Isabella Curwen and inherited the hall from Eldred Curwen in 1790, taking the name Curwen. The hall remained the home of the Curwen family until 1929 when it passed to the Chance family by marriage. At the start of the Second World War Workington Hall was requisitioned by the War Office and during military occupation suffered fire damage. Lady Chance gave the hall to Workington Council in 1945 for use as a town hall, but it fell into decay and in 1972 the decision was made to preserve it as a consolidated ruin. The Curwens retreated to Belle Isle on Windermere. John Christopher Curwen's model farm of around 1800 survives in the former park. The ruins of the hall are said to be haunted by the ghost of 'Galloping' Henry Curwen, who was murdered in his bed by a French thief. It is said that the sound of Henry's head banging on each tread of the stairs as he was dragged from the house can still be heard. The sounds of children playing and singing have also been reported.

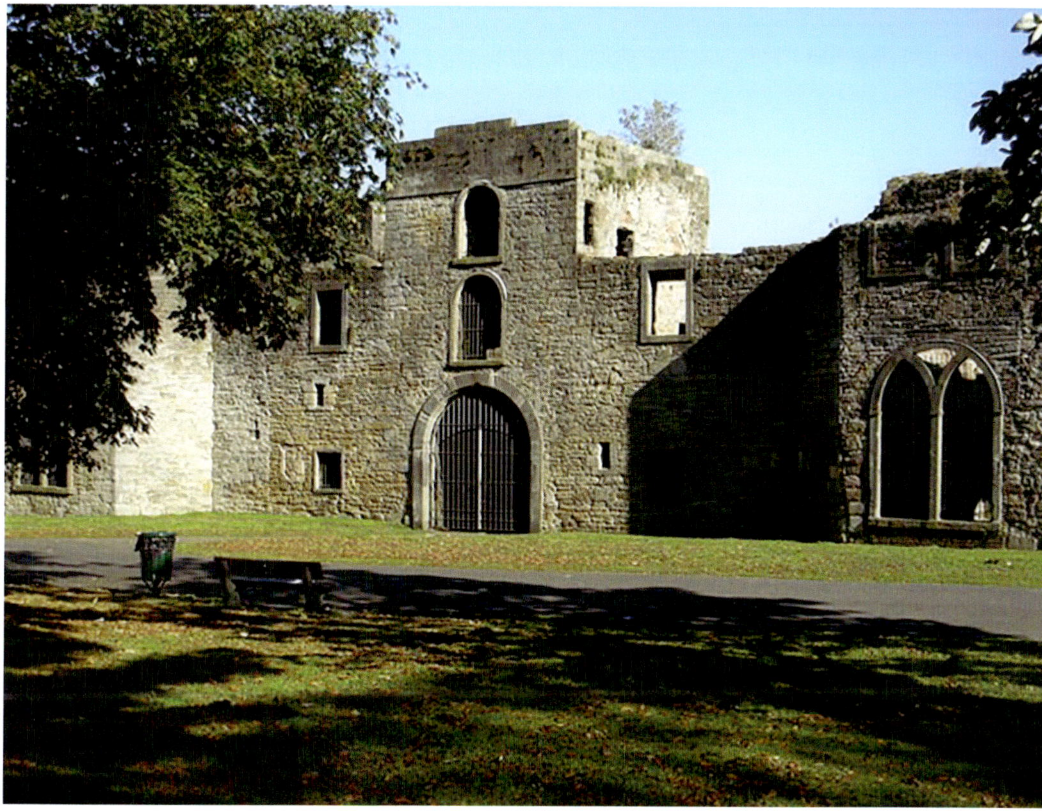

Workington Hall.

# Bibliography


Allen, Maureen, *Ireby* (MTP Media, No date).

*An Inventory of the Historical Monuments in Westmorland 1936.*

Apperley, Eric *Papcastle History* (Little Bird Publications, 2009).

Brandwood, Geoff, *The Architecture of Sharpe, Paley and Austin* (English Heritage, 2012).

Camden, William, and Gibson, Edmund, *Camden's Britannia Newly Translated into English* (London, 1695)

Curwen, John F., *A History of the Ancient House of Curwen of Workington in Cumberland and its Various Branches* (Titus Wilson and Son, 1928).

Curwen, John F., *The Later Records Relating to North Westmorland or the Barony of Appleby* (Kendal 1932).

Dalziel, Nigel and Philip, *Kirkby Lonsdale & District in Old Photographs* (Sutton Publishing, 1996).

Eastham, Paul, *People of the Sacred Valley: More Hidden Cumbrian Histories* (Fletcher Christian Publishers, 2021).

Emery, Anthony, *Greater Medieval Houses of England and Wales: Volume 1, Northern England* (Cambridge University Press, 1996).

Fermer, Val, *Ravenstonedale Tales Volume I* (The Bank House Press, 2020).

Fleming, Daniel, *Description of the Country of Westmoreland* (Bernard Quaritch, 1882).

Girouard, Mark, *Life in the English Country House* (Yale University Press, 1978).

Glyn Davies, 'New light on the Luck of Edenhall', *The Burlington Magazine* (2010).

Harrison, Philippa, *Mountain Republic* (Apollo, 2022).

Heal, Felicity, and Homes, Clive, *The Gentry in English and Wales 1500–1700* (Palgrave, 1994).

Hilton, George, and Hillman, Anne (ed.), *The Rake's Diary: The Journal of George Hilton* (Curwen Archive Texts, 1994).

Howard, Maurice, *The Early Tudor Country House: Architecture and Politics, 1490–1550* (George Philip, 1987).

Hutchinson, William, *The History of the County of Cumberland, and Some Places Adjacent, from the Earliest Accounts to the Present Time* (E. Jollie, 1794).

Hutton, William, *The Beetham Repository* (1770)

Hyde, Matthew, and Pevsner, Nikolaus, *Cumbria: Cumberland, Westmoreland and Furness*, The Buildings of England, 2nd Edition (Yale University Press, 2010).

Jefferson, Samuel, *History and Antiquities of Carlisle; With an Account of the Castels, Gentlemen's Seats, and Antiquities, in the Vicinity, and Biographical Memoirs of Eminent Men* (Samuel Jefferson and Whittaker and Company, 1838).

Jefferson, Samuel, *History and Antiquities of Carlisle; With an Account of the Castels, Gentlemen's Seats, and Antiquities, in the Vicinity, and Biographical Memoirs of Eminent Men* (1838).

Jefferson, Samuel, *The History and Antiquities of Allerdale Ward, Above Derwent, in the Country of Cumberland: With Biographical Notices and Memoirs* (1842)

Jopling, Charles M., *Sketch of Furness and Cartmel: Comprising the Hundred of Lonsdale North of the Sands* (Whittaker and Company, 1843).

Machell, Thomas, *Antiquary on Horseback* (T. Wilson, 1963).

*Mannix & Co. History, Topography and Directory of Westmorland, and of the Hundreds of Lonsdale and Amounderness in Lancashire* (W. R. Johnson, 1851).

Marshall, John, *Royal Navy Biography* (Longman, 1832).

Nicholson, Joesph, and Burn, Richard, *The History and Antiquities of the Counties of Westmorland and Cumberland* (2 vols.) (W. Strahan, T. Cadell, 1777).

Owen, Hugh, *The Lowther Family* (Phillimore, 1990).

*Oxford Dictionary of National Biography*

Philips, John, *Black's Picturesque Guide to the English Lakes* (Sadam and Charles Black, 1866).

Robinson, John Martin, *A Guide to the Country Houses of the North West* (Constable, 1991).

Salter, M., *The Castles and Tower Houses of Cumbria* (Folly Publications, 1998).

Scott, Daniel, *Bygone Cumberland and Westmorland* (William Andrews & Co., 1899).

Strong, Roy, Binney, Marcus, and Harris, John, *The Destruction of the Country House* (Thames and Hudson, 1974).

Sullivan, Jeremiah, *Cumberland and Westmoreland, Ancient and Modern: The People, Dialect, Superstitions and Customs* (Whittaker and Co., John Hudson, Jos. Dawson and Jas Robinson, 1857).

Sutherland, Douglas, *The Yellow Earl* (Merlin Unwin for Lowther Castle, 2016).

Taylor, Michael Waistell, *The Old Manorial Halls of Westmorland & Cumberland* (Titus Wilson, 1892).

Thomas, Mark, *A History of Brougham Hall and High Head Castle* (Phillimore, 1992).

Thompson, Michael, *The Decline of the Castle* (Cambridge University Press, 1987).

Toulmin Smith, Lucy (ed.), *The Itinerary of John Leland in or About the Years 1535–1543* (George Bell and Sons, 1909).

Uglow, Jenny, *The Pinecone: The Story of Sarah Losh, Romantic Heroine, Architect and Visionary* (Faber and Faber, 2012).

*Victoria County History Cumberland 2 volumes 1901 and 1905, Lancashire 8 volumes 1906–1914.*

Wasson, Ellis, *The British and Irish Ruling Class 1660–1945* (De Gruyter Open, 2017).

Worsely, Giles, *England's Lost Houses (from the Archives of Country Life)* (Aurum Press, 2002).

Wrathall, Anthony E., *Helsfell Hall: Not Just An Old Lakeland Barn* (Titus Wilson, 2021).

## Guidebooks

Lowther Castle
Lowther Caste Gardens

## Newspapers and Periodicals

*Country Life*
Cumbria Vernacular Buildings Group
*North West Evening News*
*The Whitehaven Guide*
*Times and Star*
*Transactions of the Cumberland and Westmorland Antiquarian and Archaeological Society*
*Westmoreland Gazette*
*Whitehaven News*

## Illustration Credits

The following illustrations are from my (IG) collection: *Bardsea Hall, Bolton Hall, The Biggins from the Lake, Brayton Hall (entrance front), Brougham Hall (courtyard, terrace and garden views), Brougham Hall defences, Brougham Hall (courtyard view) Crofton Hall (the arch), Dalton Hall, Eden Hall (Hall and Lodge and piers), Furness Abbey, Grizedale Hall (Garden front), Holmrook Hall, Ireby Grange (both figures), Lowther Castle (garden front) Lunefield (al figures), Nether Hall (both figures), Rheda, Whitehall (both figures) and Wood Hall, Workington Hall (entrance front and game larder)*

We have been unable to trace the copyright holder of the following illustrations but would be pleased to acknowledge them in future editions: *Englethwaite Hall, Kingmoor House, Milton Hall and Summer Grove,*

As in previous volumes I owe a considerable debt to Matthew Beckett for his kindness in allowing me to reproduce the following illustrations from his website www.lostheritage.org.uk: *Crofton Hall (entrance front), Eden Hall, Ewanrigg Hall (oblique view), Grimeshill, High Biggins (garden front),* and *High Head Castle (entrance front),*

The illustrations of *Beetham Hall* (by John Darch), *Hardrigg Hall* (by Matthew Hatton) *High Head Castle, aerial view* (by Simon Ledingham), *Killington Hall (*by Alan Murray-Rust*) and Raw Head* (*gateposts*) (by Karl and Ali) are used with grateful thanks under the Creative Commons licence. Val Fermer couldn't have been more helpful in answering my questions and providing me with a copy of the sales brochure for Hwith.

The images of *Abbot's Wood (the saloon)*, *Brandlinghill, Brayton Hall reconstructed after the fire, Brayton Hall ruins, Eden Hall (entrance front), Englethwaite Hall (colour photograph), Ewanrigg (main block), Fell Foot House, Gilgarron House, Helsfell Hall, Killhow, Kirklinton (ruins), Lamplugh, Maulds Meaburn Hall, Middleton Hall, Netherhall (derelict), Netherhall (Roman remains), Rheda (distant view), Ribton Hall, Warwick Hall, Wharton Hall, Woodside Hall (Georgian house)* and *Workington Hall (the saloon)* are from the Cumbrian Image Bank and reproduced with the kind permission of Cumbria County Council Libraries. I am enormously grateful to Carolyn White and Carla Horner for their kind assistance in locating these images. The image of the Luck of Edenhall is reproduced by kind permission of the Victoria and Albert Museum. Thomas Machell's drawing of Lowther Castle is reproduced by permission of Lowther Castle Ltd with thanks to Charlotte Fairbairn for her assistance.

The illustrations of *Brayton Hall (Garden Front)*, *Brayton Hall (smaller house after the fire) Brayton Hall (entrance and garden fronts), Brayton Hall in 1920, Grizedale Hall (entrance front), Hartley Castle, High Head Castle (Samuel and Nathaniel Buck), Holmrook Hall (engraving), Lowther Hall (Kip), Lowther Hall (Campbells proposals), Hugh Lowether, Woodside, Wharton Hall (1773), Workington Hall (entrance front)* are, as far as we have been able to establish, in the public domain.

*Crofton Hall (the staircase)* is reproduced from the Crofton Hall website with their kind permission (www.croftonhall.co.uk). Those of *Grange Hall, Helsfell Hall* and *Cunswick Hall* are reproduced by kind permission of the Armitt Trust and with thanks to Sue Osman.

The painting of *Lunefield, Roger Carus' House* is reproduced with the permission of the Archive Service Manager, Lancashire Archives.

The images of Abbotts Wood, Barrow House, Brougham Castle from the road, Netherhall (distant view) and Oak Lea are from the Sankey Photographic Collection and Cumbria Archives at Barrow and I am most grateful to Susan Benson, archivist at the Cumbria Archive Centre for her assistance.

The illustration of *Bryerswood* is from The Builder (1888) and of Hartley Castle from Legends and Historical Notes of North Westmoreland by Thomas Gibson (1887). The engraving of Brougham Hall is from History of the County of Cumberland by William Hutchinson (1794) and the drawing of Bardsea Hall (1843) from A Sketch of Furness and Cartmel.

I would like to offer my thanks to Anthony Wrathall for his assistance with the Helsfell entry.